ITALIAN TEXTS AND STUDIES ON RELIGION AND SOCIETY

Edmondo Lupieri, *General Editor*

Italian religious history has been pivotal to the formation and growth of European and Western civilization and cultures. Unfortunately, many texts which are fundamental for the understanding of its importance have long remained inaccessible to non-Italian readers. Similarly, the exciting developments of Italian scholarship in the field of the studies of religion have not always come into the public eye outside of Italy. Particularly since the end of World War II there has been continuous expansion in the field, and currently Italian scholars are combining the old and solid Italian tradition of philological and historical studies with new and innovative ideas and methodologies.

Italian Texts and Studies on Religion and Society (ITSORS) is a new series. Its publications are all English translations of works originally published or composed in Italy. The main aim of ITSORS is to have readers in the English-speaking world become acquainted with Italian socio-religious history and with the best of Italian scholarly research on religion with socio-historical implications. For this reason ITSORS will have two branches: *Texts* and *Studies*.

Texts consist of classical works and are intended to be useful as sources for a better comprehension of important events in Western religious history. Many are not readily available or have never been translated into English. *Studies* comprise original works of the best contemporary Italian scholarship which offer methodological contributions to research and make inroads into seldom studied areas.

BOOKS PUBLISHED

Odoric of Pordenone
The Travels of Friar Odoric
(Sponsored by the Chamber of Commerce of Pordenone, Italy)

Edmondo Lupieri
The Mandaeans: The Last Gnostics
(Sponsored by the Italian Ministry of Foreign Affairs)

Bruno Forte
The Essence of Christianity

Bruno Forte
To Follow You, Light of Life

To Follow You, Light of Life

SPIRITUAL EXERCISES PREACHED BEFORE
JOHN PAUL II AT THE VATICAN

Bruno Forte

Translated by

David Glenday

William B. Eerdmans Publishing Company

Grand Rapids, Michigan / Cambridge, U.K.

Originally published in Italian under the title
Seguendo Te, luce della vita, by Mondadori, Milano, 2004.

This English edition
© 2005 Wm. B. Eerdmans Publishing Co.

Wm. B. Eerdmans Publishing Co.
255 Jefferson Ave. S.E., Grand Rapids, Michigan 49503 /
P.O. Box 163, Cambridge CB3 9PU U.K.

Printed in the United States of America

10 09 08 07 06 05   7 6 5 4 3 2 1

Library of Congress Cataloging-in-Publication Data

Forte, Bruno.
To follow You, Light of Life: spiritual exercises preached before John Paul II at the Vatican /
Bruno Forte; translated by David Glenday.
    p.   cm.   — (Italian texts and studies on religion and society)
Includes bibliographical references and index.
ISBN-10: 0-8028-2935-X / ISBN-13: 978-0-8028-2935-1 (pbk.: alk. paper)
1. Spiritual retreats for clergy — Catholic Church.   2. Spiritual exercises.
3. Sermons, Italian — Translations into English.   4. Catholic Church — Sermons.
I. Title.   II. Series.

BX1912.5.F68   2005
269'.692 — dc22

2005050713

www.eerdmans.com

Gathered in this book are the meditations preached by me in the Vatican, before the Holy Father John Paul II and his closest aides, from February 29 to March 6, 2004. The meditations are introduced by the letter which the Pope was kind enough to address to me at the conclusion of the six-day retreat, and which he chose himself to read in the presence of all those who had participated.

I dedicate these pages to the dear memory of my sister Ida, who went to meet the Lord only a short time before the retreat began: I am certain that her sufferings and faith helped prepare for the retreat, and that her intercession with God, the light of her life and mine, sustained and accompanied the prayer of those days.

Contents

CONTENTS

Foreword

To Reverend Monsignor
BRUNO FORTE

Dear Professor,
It gives me great pleasure to express my heartfelt gratitude to you at the conclusion of these Spiritual Exercises, during which you have guided us in the contemplation of the mystery who is Christ by offering us a series of profound reflections on the theme: "To Follow You, Light of Life."

I think with great appreciation of the work involved for you in preparing this retreat, both earlier and nearer to the time. Both I myself and those who work with me in the Roman Curia have drawn advantage from the reflections you have offered us with such originality of insight and wide theological, biblical and spiritual knowledge. We have also been struck by the passion with which you have presented your reflections, repeatedly making reference to the everyday experiences of your life as a priest. We are grateful to you because, in the style which characterizes your theological research and pastoral ministry, you have offered our minds and hearts points which are of considerable importance if we desire to follow with ever renewed commitment the One who is the Light of the world.

Finally, I would like to express to you my special appreciation of the conversational yet prayerful tone which you have imparted to this pilgrimage of ours, helping us to lift our spirits up to God in that contemplative attitude, pervaded with faith and love, to which I never cease calling the People of God, exhorting Christian communities to shine in the midst of the world above all in the "art of prayer" (cf. *Novo millennio ineunte,* 32).

The Lord, for His part, will know to reward you for all this, and I entrust you and your zealous and faithful service to the Church to Him. May the Blessed Virgin Mary, whom you have helped us contemplate in the context of our earthly pilgrimage towards our home in heaven, watch over you and your entire ministry. As for me, I assure you of a special remembrance in my prayers, while I impart to you my Apostolic Blessing, which I gladly extend to all the persons dear to you.

JOANNES PAULUS II
from the Vatican, March 6, 2004

Opening Greeting

Holy Father!

It is a very great honor for me to preach this retreat to you and your closest aides: for this grace I thank God, in whose presence we shall live during these days spent together, and I thank you, too, because by the fact of calling me to this task you have given me the confidence to believe that I can carry it out with the Lord's help.

Together with my gratitude, I would like to express my very deep love for you personally. In this way, I would like also to act as the spokesperson of all those who have promised to support my ministry during these days by their sacrifice and prayer: men and women living the cloistered and contemplative life, bishops and priests, consecrated persons, missionaries, laypeople, the elderly and sick, couples and whole families, adults, young people and children, all those to whom in one way or another I am bound by my priestly ministry.

We will also have the prayers of many of my fellow theologians and of my students: by sharing in this retreat in this way, they demonstrate that doing theology, a vocation that comes from God, is intimately bound to the fact of our being part of the church. Inasmuch as this science is no aristocratic "love of wisdom," but rather the humble "wisdom of love," seeking to give expression to a love that is lived, theology stands or falls with the cross of Christ, where this love revealed itself for us, and it lives in the communion of the church, where it is touched and nourished by God's love.

We will, finally, be accompanied by that "cloud of witnesses" (Heb. 12:1), to whom I will be making frequent reference, and on whose help I call from the start, beginning with Mary, the Mother of the Redeemer, to whose maternal intercession I entrust everything.

Sustained by so great help, I have special confidence in the state of grace connected to the invitation received from you, Holy Father, and also expressed in the warm welcome accorded to me by all of you, Eminent Cardinals, Most Reverend Archbishops, Bishops and brothers in baptism and the priesthood: I invite all of you to pray so that the Holy Spirit may make use of me as one day he made use of the jawbone of Balaam's ass, notwithstanding the resistance offered by that somewhat unusual prophet (cf. Num. 22:22-35 and 2 Pet. 2:15-16).

BRUNO FORTE

Introduction

In this introduction I intend to respond to four questions: First, what are the "spiritual exercises"? Second, where do they start from? Third, what is their purpose? And fourth, in whose company are they to be undertaken?

The "Spiritual Exercises"

Both in the church's spiritual tradition and in its ongoing experience, the "spiritual exercises" are perhaps best understood as a time given us by God so that we may in our turn return it to him with sincere love: a time, that is, spent listening reverently to his Word and guarded by his silence, so as to come to know the truth about who we truly are in his presence and attain ever greater personal conformity to his will. St. Ignatius of Loyola, the father and first teacher of the exercises, affirms that the aim of those who do them must be to "conquer oneself and regulate one's life" *("vencer a sí mismo y ordenar su vida"),* thus achieving in ever increasing measure the end for which the human person is created: "to praise, reverence, and serve God our Lord" *("alabar, hacer reverencia y servir a Dios nuestro Señor").*[1]

They are called "exercises" because they call for serious and persever-

---

1. St. Ignatius of Loyola, *Spiritual Exercises* 21, 23.

1

ing commitment in terms of several periods of intense prayer distributed throughout the day and over several days. These times of prayer are spent in an attitude of attentiveness, understanding, judgment, and decision, with the help of some rather straightforward suggestions about how to meditate and discern. They are called "spiritual" because at work in them above all is the Holy Spirit. It is to him that our spirit is invited to open itself in docility and freedom, so as to know that love of God which the Spirit himself pours into our hearts (cf. Rom. 5:5). Without the Spirit, the exercises could be neither undertaken nor understood.

The complete form of the exercises — from which we will take inspiration for our own — is that set down by St. Ignatius of Loyola, who had long experienced them in his own life before going on to offer them to others as a particularly helpful journey toward conversion and personal renewal. In this Ignatian form, the use of the exercises has been recommended by the church on a number of occasions. In 1929, for example, Pope Pius XI dedicated to them his encyclical *Mens nostra*. In this letter, he laid down that the exercises should be "given" each year in the Vatican, as an example for all and a gift to himself and his closest aides. The reasons why the church has shown such special favor toward the exercises may be more clearly understood if we consider their starting point, the journey that they propose be undertaken, and the destination to which they lead, together with the spiritual climate and conditions in which they are done. It is to these matters that I now wish to turn.

The Landscape of the Exercises: Where Do We Start From?

The landscape in which the exercises are situated is none other than that "history of salvation" in which are inscribed the life and mission of each one of us, the church we love, and the human family to which we belong. Three words can help to describe this landscape — "garden," "desert," and "word."

We could say that, in the beginning, according to the Bible, God was the gardener. As the story is told at the opening of the book of Genesis, God labored for six days to make *a garden* (Hebrew: *gan;* the Greek and

Latin words indicate "paradise") where everything was beautiful (*tov,* meaning both good and beautiful), and where at the same time every single thing was at one with all the others, while remaining distinct from them, in a wonderful harmony at the summit of which stood the human person, the guardian of paradise.

Sin transforms this garden into *a desert* (Hebrew: *midbar*), the arid ground that fallen Adam would have to till by the sweat of his brow. This is why the sense of longing expectation evoked by God's promise of salvation expresses itself in the vision of a time when the desert will flower and the earth will once again be the garden of God: "until a spirit from on high is poured out on us, and the wilderness becomes a fruitful field" (Isa. 32:15). Then the new shoot will sprout — and this shoot will be the Messiah himself (cf. Isa. 11:1).

The power that will transform the desert into a garden is *the word* (Hebrew: *dabar*). This word will vanquish the desert and cause life to flower there again. The play on the words *midbar* and *dabar* — so dear to the rabbinic tradition — expresses the dramatic struggle that lies at the heart of Israel's hope, and so also at the heart of the hope of the church, of which Israel is the "holy root" (Rom. 11:16-18). Only the Word of the living God will turn the earth made lifeless by sin into a garden full of the new delights celebrated in the Song of Songs. To achieve its mission, the Word — coming down from on high like rain (cf. Isa. 55:10) — will have to disappear into the earth. Then it will give life to the desert of the world and to the desert of our hearts, as the prophets had foretold: "I will now allure her, and bring her into the wilderness, and speak tenderly to her" (Hos. 2:14).

It is against this backdrop that we can understand why the intensely rich symbolism of the Fourth Gospel places the world's new beginning in a garden, and why the woman who goes to the tomb takes the Risen One for a "gardener," the caretaker of God's new garden (cf. John 20:15). The divine, incarnate, and now exalted Word thus reestablishes and renews the beauty of the origins. Today, as in every age, the human heart needs this Word more than the very air we breathe.

Indeed, after the collapse of so many myths that have played out afresh the drama of the first sin on a dramatic and global scale, the human heart perhaps needs this Word more today than at any other time in history. After the season of "light" — the age of the heady ideologies that recognized in reason alone the ability to transform the world and life — the violence produced by the historical forms taken by those ideologies has brought humankind to an experience of deep darkness. This is the "night of the world" of which Martin Heidegger spoke: the darkness of this night is not so much the absence of God as the fact that human beings feel nothing for this absence. This is the night of nihilism, that indifference to eternal values which corrodes the very capacity of human beings to set out in search of the meaning of life and history. It is the condition expressed by the rabbinic saying quoted by Martin Buber: "Israel's real exile began when the Jews learnt how to bear that exile." Exile does not begin when we leave home, but when we no longer miss it. We can emerge from the night of exile only by rekindling in our hearts the passionate longing for home. This is what happens every time the Word is proclaimed, sending us back to search for lost meaning and pointing to the dawning of the new day.

This especially is what is required of the church today: at this time of the world's night, of the crisis of modern utopias and postmodern disillusionment, in this world often perceived as scarred by the clash of civilizations and religions, the church is called more than ever before to make the desert of the world and of our hearts flower again so as to become God's new garden.

Thus it is that the garden and the desert provide the landscape of our exercises, as well as their starting point. Here we hear the call to seek the Word so as to make the desert in and around us flower afresh.

Journey and Destination: Jesus Christ, the Light of Life

This Word is Jesus the Christ: he is both our journey and our destination in these spiritual exercises. Jesus himself is the Word able to transform our desert into the garden that we have been promised and for which we long; he is the light that the world needs to emerge from the darkness that otherwise would envelop all things: "I am the light of the world. Whoever follows me will never walk in darkness but will have the light of life" (John 8:12).

We are led into a deeper understanding of what these words mean by the Transfiguration, when this is read in the light of an ancient rabbinic tradition according to which in the beginning Adam was clothed in light (Hebrew: *'wr*); it was only with the appearance of sin that this light was covered by the skin of fallen man (Hebrew for "skin": *'wr*, which only adds an initial aspirate to the *'wr* of light). When the Messiah comes, this skin, this veil, will once more make way for the light of the beginnings: the new Adam will be the Adam of light.

This is what happens on the mountain of Transfiguration: "His face shone like the sun, and his clothes became dazzling white" (Matt. 17:2). On Tabor, Jesus shows that he is the new Adam, in shining light, dwelling in God's new garden. So it is that the Transfiguration becomes the door to saving beauty: "Lord, it is good for us to be here; if you wish, I will make three dwellings here, one for you, one for Moses, and one for Elijah" (Matt. 17:4). To experience the exercises will thus mean to experience here and now in the Spirit the gift first given on Tabor: to go up the mountain, to let ourselves be flooded with God's light, and to come down again, transfigured by the One who is light from light, so as to be his witnesses before our fellow women and men. This, then, is the purpose, the destination, of these exercises: to dispose ourselves to receive the grace of transfiguration on God's mountain and in Jesus' company.

To come to know Jesus, to welcome his light into our deepest selves, to fall ever more in love with him, the rule and hope of our lives, to let ourselves be molded in his image by his living Spirit — this is the goal to which our journey tends. The exercises aim at nothing other than our becoming, ever more radically, disciples of the One who said: "I am the light of the world. Whoever follows me will never walk in darkness but will have the light of life" (John 8:12).

Thus it is that we will walk with Jesus in the choices he made in his life, in lively remembrance of his journey of freedom toward the cross and the dawn of Easter, so as to let ourselves be flooded by the Spirit poured out by him, who alone can make us free. This will be our *via purificativa*: this will be the way we walk on the first day of the exercises — the day of freedom. We will climb the mountain, to experience the mercy that saves, the gift of our heavenly Father (*deformata reformare*). Thus his promise will be fulfilled: "Whoever follows me *will never walk in darkness*. . . ."

Then we will walk with Jesus toward the Cross, pausing with him on Tabor: this will be our *via illuminativa,* which in the darkness of Good Friday will bring us to know the light that enlightens every human being and that will flood our hearts and lives, too, so that we may be conformed to him *(reformata conformare).* This will be the second day — the day of the cross: "I am the light of the world. *Whoever follows me* will never walk in darkness. . . ."

Then we will let ourselves be drawn by the splendor of the Easter revelation: this will be our *via unitiva,* which will lead us to live with Christ in God the last three days of our retreat — the day of Easter, the day of the church, and the day of mission *(conformata confirmare; confirmata transformare),* coming down from the mountain of the Transfiguration so that the word of Jesus may be fulfilled in us: "Whoever follows me will never walk in darkness *but will have the light of life.*"

The contemplation of the mysteries of our Savior — which each day will occupy the two morning meditations — will be the door to life for us: the beauty of the One who is "the beautiful Shepherd" *(ho poimēn ho kalos:* John 10:11) will become ours too, because we will be able to come to know ourselves hidden with him in the beauty of God (cf. Col. 3:3). We will also be able to say with Peter on the mountain, and with Peter present among us: "Lord, it is good for us to be here. . . ."

Who Will Walk with Us?

In this journey of transfiguration with and in Christ we will not walk alone; as our traveling companions we will have that "cloud of witnesses" (Heb. 12:1), who like us have encountered the Lord and become his disciples, beloved in the Beloved. Each day the two afternoon meditations will lead us to encounter in the Bible some of those who witness to the faith that changes lives, so as to learn from them to do what they did and walk together in the way of Jesus. They will help us to climb our own Tabor, to remain there in the light of the Transfiguration, and to come down the mountain toward the future God is preparing for us. In the saints it is the gospel that speaks, the Word of salvation written not on tablets of stone but on hearts of flesh beating with life. They will be our companions. To them — to those of whom we will speak, as well as to all the others of whom we will not — we entrust our exercises, so that they may intercede for us to obtain the grace of that conversion of heart out of which shines the light of the beauty that saves.

In a unique and excellent way, however, from among all this "cloud of witnesses" shines forth Mary, the All Holy, the Virgin Mother of the Beloved, the Spouse of the new and eternal covenant. In her, the first and the new covenants meet, and in her we are promised and granted a foretaste of future glory: she is the Daughter of Zion, the Ark of the Covenant, the Queen of heaven. In the *lectio divina* at the conclusion of each day of our exercises, we will turn our hearts and minds to her. To Mary, "sanctuary and resting-place of the blessed Trinity,"[2] this woman in whom is reflected, as in an icon, the entire mystery of our redemption, to her whom "all generations will call blessed" (Luke 1:48), we entrust our exercises.

We ask her especially to help us accept the conditions necessary so that the grace experienced here may bear abundant fruit, mirroring in some way what she experienced when she let the Spirit come upon her. In the church's spiritual tradition these conditions have been expressed with the threefold formula of *totus introibo, solus manebo,* and *alius egrediar.* We enter these exercises with our whole being, bearing with us all the challenges that may be troubling us and the hard things that make us suffer, as Mary did when the angel visited her: *Totus introibo.* Then, in the exercises we will remain alone before God alone, like Mary at the annunciation, attentive guardians of the silence in which resounds that Word of life before which we are called to make our decisions. No one can make for me the decisions I am called to make regarding my eternal salvation and my vocation to serve my fellow women and men: *Solus manebo.* In this way, the miracle of the Transfiguration can happen here and now, and we will be able to emerge from these exercises as new creatures, different from what is old in us, new according to the Adam of light that Christ has made of us, and of whom he has given us an image and a model in the woman Mary: *Alius egrediar.* With her, we will ask her Son, the light of the world, to welcome

2. St. Louis M. Grignion de Montfort, *Trattato della vera devozione alla Santa Vergine,* 5.

us back renewed among his followers, sealing us in these days with the fire
of his Spirit of love:

Lord Jesus Christ,
Son of God, Redeemer of humankind,
send your Spirit upon us
to help us experience these exercises
in truth and freedom,
    following you, light of life!
Grant us the purification of our hearts,
    following you, light of life!
Lead us to understand the Father's will for us,
    following you, light of life!
Make us new so that we may do his will,
    following you, light of life!
Let us be your witnesses,
    following you, light of life!
Lead us to contemplate eternal beauty,
    following you, light of life!
Because you alone are the light of the world,
you alone the light of our lives,
now in the hour of our journeying
and always,
in the day of the light that never dies.
Amen! Alleluia!

"I am the light of the world. Whoever walks in me will never walk in darkness but will have the light of life."

John 8:12

CALLED TO FREEDOM

This first day of our retreat — the "day of freedom" — corresponds to the *via purificativa* of the spiritual exercises: it aims at the reformation of our hearts and lives (*deformata reformare,* a decisive reformation of whatever might be separating us from God and keeping us far from him). The intention is, as it were, to hold our deepest choices up against those of Jesus, as we walk with him in his own journey of freedom. After all, it was he himself who promised: "Whoever follows me will never walk in darkness but will have the light of life" (John 8:12).

We call on our Savior using the prayer St. Ignatius of Loyola set at the head of his *Spiritual Exercises,* a prayer that expresses the fundamental idea that inspires these exercises and the journey they essentially entail:

> Soul of Christ, sanctify me.
> Body of Christ, save me.
> Blood of Christ, inebriate me.
> Water from the side of Christ, wash me.
> Passion of Christ, strengthen me.
> O good Jesus, hear me;
> Within thy wounds, hide me;
> Suffer me not to be separated from thee;
> From the malignant enemy defend me;
> In the hour of my death call me;

And bid me to come to thee,
That with thy saints I may praise thee
Forever and ever. Amen.

1

Jesus, a Story of Freedom:
The Choice He Made and the Way He Lived

Was Jesus free? Was the story of his life made up of real alternatives and choices, in facing which he defined his life and mission? Or — because of his divine condition — had everything been decided for him in advance, only to be played out as a faithful reflection of God's eternal choice? The way we answer these questions makes a very great difference to the picture we have of Jesus and how we follow him.

The faith of the church has given our questions here a definitive answer: the condemnation of those who came to affirm that in Christ there was only one will (the "monothelists" at the Third Council of Constantinople in 681) affirmed that without a shadow of a doubt Jesus was indeed endowed with human will and freedom, that he was a free person who chose his future under no constraint, and who accepted and took upon himself all the risks involved in freedom.

Did such risks involve the possibility of a conflict between his condition as the Son who is the Word living in the Father's presence and his condition as a human person living among other human persons? Would Jesus have been able to say no to God's plan so as to follow his own, and thus to sin? To these questions, too, from the earliest days the faith of the church has given its answer, strongly affirming that "he committed no sin" (1 Pet. 2:22). "We have one who in every respect has been tested as we are, yet without sin" (Heb. 4:15). This was precisely the way Jesus broke the hold exercised by sin and caused the new life coming from above to break into the story of each one of us. So Paul can say: "For our sake he made him to be sin who knew no sin, so that in him we might become the righteousness of God" (2 Cor. 5:21). Nevertheless, this incontrovertible fact must not distort the way we read the human story of the Christ. The fact that he did not know sin does not mean that as a human person he did not know the risk and struggle involved in being free. In fact, it was precisely in the midst of the tribulations of the flesh that the Son, sent in sinful flesh to condemn sin in the flesh (cf. Rom. 8:3), chose the path of unconditional faithfulness to the Father.

May we thus speak in Jesus' case of a real history of freedom, a journey from one choice to another along the narrow path of obedience to God? If so, what shape did this story take? What were its main stages? As in the story of every human being, so also in the experience of the Son who came in the flesh, a distinction has to be made between the various levels of freedom. First of all, there is the freedom exercised in the deepest reaches of one's conscience, which radically affects every subsequent decision. This happens at the deep level of what may be called the fundamental option, the radical choice of life's ultimate horizon, capable of giving meaning and unity to the many decisions subsequently to be taken in the various areas of one's life. In this fundamental choice are to be found the ultimate motivation and unifying criterion of the many choices; here the truth of a person's existence finds expression, or — in biblical terms — here we show what is in our "heart."

At its very deepest level, the fundamental option is motivated by our natural desire to be completely fulfilled, which — in the understanding of the great Christian tradition — is our natural desire to see God. In this sense, a life's radical option may be authentic or inauthentic, fulfilling or alienating, according to whether or not it is in harmony with our longing for the Eternal One inscribed in our hearts. The quality of our fundamental option thus finds expression in our choice of the end and the means to ensure the fulfillment of our ultimate desire. Here the beautiful etymology of the word "desire" reveals its full meaning. The Latin root of the word means being far from the stars and aspiring to reach them, like a soothsayer gazing at the starry sky (*desideribus*); it has to do with our longing for the presence of the Absent One.

In this sense, the human heart made for God is pure desire: "You made us for yourself, and our hearts are restless until they rest in you."[1] The fundamental option, motivated by the desire each of us has in our deepest being, attains fulfillment in the down-to-earth reality of the many decisions we take moment by moment. This is the second level of freedom: "situated" or "engaged" freedom, that freedom lived out in the tension between the openness of the radical choice and the finitude of the possibilities present in each particular concrete situation.

The totality of our concrete choices and the way they are related to our fundamental option indicate our way of life, that complex of constant characteristics in which the infinite openness of our desire comes up against the concrete reality of experience and is determined with respect to it. If our fundamental option is in harmony with our innate desire for self-fulfillment, and if our subsequent individual choices are faithful to this option, then our journey of freedom becomes a journey of being freed, of liberation from what makes us less human, toward that which fulfills and enhances our true humanity. If not, our lives become an experience of being alienated from our true selves. The story of the freedom of each human person can thus be a story of liberation or of alienation.

What was the experience of Jesus of Nazareth at these different levels of freedom? Did he choose a fundamental option? If so, what was it? How did Jesus live out the choices called for by the concrete relationships of which his existence was woven? What was his way of life?

The Fundamental Option of Jesus of Nazareth: The Kingdom of God

Jesus' fundamental option can be discerned in everything he did, but it finds particularly clear expression in some key moments of his life. Among these, two in particular — situated respectively at the beginning and end of his public ministry — reveal him to be engaged in making his decisive

---

1. St. Augustine, *Confessiones* 1.1: *"Fecisti nos ad te et inquietum est cor nostrum, donec requiescat in te."*

choice when faced respectively with life and death: we speak here of the "mystery" of the *temptations in the desert* and of the *agony in Gethsemane.*

Jesus' temptations have been most commonly interpreted as a kind of didactic exercise. In them, it is said, the Lord showed us how we in our turn should overcome temptation — but without being really tempted himself. This way of explaining the temptations was intended to avoid any risk of diminishing Jesus' divine perfection. Yet excessive insistence on this didactic aspect of Christ's temptations runs the risk of depriving them of any real seriousness. Jesus would have just gone through the motions, even if for the commendable purpose of giving us instruction. His would thus not be a truly human story, but — as Jacques Maritain would say — a kind of "parody of humanity."

Of course, the didactic value of the temptations must not be set aside, but it holds only if the temptations are indeed real. In fact, various New Testament witnesses are at hand to confirm their reality. Jesus himself speaks of his "trials" (Luke 22:28: the term used is the very one used for the temptations, *peirasmos*). "Because he himself was tested by what he suffered," says the letter to the Hebrews, "he is able to help those who are being tested" (Heb. 2:18). In the temptations he "learned obedience": "In the days of his flesh, Jesus offered up prayers and supplications, with loud cries and tears, to the one who was able to save him from death, and he was heard because of his reverent submission. Although he was a Son, he learned obedience through what he suffered" (Heb. 5:7-8).

Further, the very fact that Matthew and Luke replace Mark's bare account (1:12-13) with the presentation of the three temptations (Matt. 4:1-11; Luke 4:1-13), developed in parallel with Israel's own temptations in the desert, shows how the early community understood that this episode represented a real choice, a kind of decisive turning point, summing up the whole history of salvation: the fullness of time had come. Just as Israel was really tested, so Jesus is truly tempted: the context is the same — the desert of overwhelming aloneness with God. The indication of time is equally charged with theological significance, the forty days, bringing to mind the forty years of the Exodus and the time spent by Moses on the mountain (cf. Exod. 24:18 and 34:28); there are three temptations, corresponding to the trials experienced by the chosen people.

The hunger of Israel and their grumbling against God, to which the Eternal One responds with the gift of manna (cf. Exod. 16 and Num. 11), correspond to the devil's invitation to Jesus to change the stones into bread (cf. Matt. 4:3 and Luke 4:3). Jesus' reply recalls the interpretation of this first temptation of Israel offered by the book of Deuteronomy: "He humbled you . . . in order to make you understand that one does not live by bread alone, but by every word that comes from the mouth of God" (8:3). The thirst of Israel and their protest at Massah, which leads Moses to sin by putting God to the test (cf. Exod. 17:1-7; Num. 20:2-13), corresponds to the devil's suggestion to Jesus of constraining God to do a miracle (cf. Matt. 4:6). Here, Jesus' reply recalls the admonition explicitly related to the episode of the waters of Massah: "Do not put the Lord your God to the test" (Deut. 6:16). Finally, the temptation of replacing the true God with an idol (whether the golden calf [cf. Exod. 32], or the gods of Canaan [cf. Exod. 23:20-33; 34:11-14]), corresponds to the devil's offer: "All these I will give you, if you will fall down and worship me" (Matt. 4:9). Once again, Jesus' reply recalls the teaching of Deuteronomy: "The Lord your God you shall fear; him you shall serve, and by his name alone you shall swear" (6:13). Thus Jesus in the desert relived the temptations of the chosen people; however, where Israel succumbed, Jesus triumphed.

The comparison between the more developed accounts offered by Matthew and Luke, and Mark's simpler version, however, leads one to suppose that there is in fact only one real temptation. This is the supreme challenge that seduced the first Adam: to trust in oneself and the power of the world instead of in God and his "weakness." This is the radical alternative: "love of self till God is forgotten, or love of God till self is forgotten."[2] Jesus experiences temptation's seductive pull, the apparently superior effectiveness it promises: on the one hand, he knows the fascination of the political and worldly messianism of his time, encountered among his people as he shared their suffering under oppression; on the other, he chooses the messianism of prophetic obedience, which he had come to know in his conversations with the Father, and especially through reading the

---

2. St. Augustine, *De Civitate Dei* 14.28: "*Amor sui usque ad contemptum Dei — amor Dei usque ad contemptum sui.*"

Scriptures about the suffering Servant and the prophets. Jesus does not seek easy consensus or pander to people's expectations, but rather subverts them. Jesus chooses the Father: with an act of sovereign freedom he prefers obedience to God and abnegation of self over obedience to self, which would imply the rejection of God. He does not succumb to the pull of immediate success; he believes in the Father with indestructible confidence. In the hour of temptation, Jesus reaffirms his freedom from himself, free for the Father and for others, free with the freedom of love.

"The devil," writes Luke (4:13), "departed from him until an opportune time," indicating that the struggle against the devil ran through the whole of Jesus' earthly story. Truly, Jesus' life is "one long, incisive discernment of spirits" (H. Urs von Balthasar), until the final hour in Jerusalem when Jesus is in Gethsemane, at the end of his journey, at the moment when he stands before the ultimate consequence of his choice of love. He experiences — to the point of sweating blood (cf. Luke 22:44) — the whole weight of the testing that he is called to live. The evangelists speak of his anguish (cf. Mark 14:33 and Matt. 26:37), his sadness (Mark 14:34 and Matt. 26:38), and his fear (Mark 14:33). He feels the very human need for the company of his friends: "Remain here; and stay awake with me" (Matt. 26:38). But he is left alone, tremendously alone, facing his future, as happens to all of us when we are called to make life's fundamental choices: "Could you not stay awake with me one hour?" (Matt 26:40). Yet again he is faced, in the most violent of ways, with the radical alternative: to save his own life or lose it, to choose between his own will and the Father's: "Abba, Father, for you all things are possible; remove this cup from me" (Mark 14:36 and parallels). At the moment when he confirms the "yes" of his radical freedom, he clings totally to the Father and calls to him with the name of trust and tenderness: "Abba, . . . yet, not what I want, but what you want." It is not by chance that this is the only time that the Gospels preserve Jesus' use of the affectionate Aramaic form *Abba* in addressing the Father. Jesus' yes is born of unconditional love: his freedom is the freedom of love, the freedom of one who finds his life by losing it (cf. Mark 8:35), able to risk everything for love. It is the daring of one who gives all.

In these mysteries of Jesus' life, his fundamental option finds transparent expression. This is the choice on which he wagers everything. The author of the letter to the Hebrews interpreted it by using the words of Psalm 40:9(8): "See, I have come to do your will" (Heb. 10:9). "My food," says Christ in the Gospel of John, "is to do the will of him who sent me and to complete his work" (John 4:34; cf. 8:29; 15:10). At the deepest level of his freedom, Jesus is a person totally free to love, entirely focused on the Father and on others. He witnesses to how none are freer than those who are free from their own freedom in the name of a greater love. Free from self, he exists for the Father and for others: he is not concerned with self-promotion, but with promoting God and his Kingdom among men and women. This is his fundamental option, which really makes him "the free man." To live for the Kingdom of God that is coming is the meaning of his life.

The Way Jesus Lived: Being Poor

How does Jesus live out this fundamental option of his in the many individual choices of his life? How does the *way he lived* take shape in the light of the supreme choice he made? The most intense form in which Jesus expresses his fundamental option in his behavior is his poverty. This poverty of his is certainly not a passive thing, certainly not that condition of misery to which a person's life may be subjected, and which was perceived throughout the history of Israel as a scandal and punishment from which the Eternal One desires to free us (cf. Deut. 15:4). Instead, Jesus freely chooses poverty to express his radical freedom and unconditional trust in the Father; it is an active poverty, in the spirit of the tradition of the "poor of God" (cf. Ps. 74:19; 149:4-5), friends and servants of the Lord (cf. Ps 86:1-2), who take refuge in him with love and reverence (cf. Ps. 34:5-11). Jesus is poor because he places his cause unconditionally in the hands of the Father (cf. Jer. 20:12-13), in boundless freedom from self, from the riches of this world, and from others. Free from self, he is "gentle and humble in heart" (Matt. 11:29) and lives in total obedience to the Father (cf. John 4:34; 5:19ff.; etc.).

Free of possessions, Jesus was born poor (in Bethlehem; cf. Luke 2:7); he lived poor (in Nazareth; cf. Matt. 13:55); he acted in absolute poverty, without even a place "to lay his head" (Matt. 8:20); and he died poor, without even the last sign of personal property, his clothes (Matt. 27:35). Free from others, he is pure in heart: he draws near to others not to possess or use them, but to love them as they are and to give himself disinterestedly to them. He is among his own "as one who serves" (Luke 22:27). "The Son of Man came not to be served but to serve, and to give his life as a ransom for many" (Matt. 20:28).

A particularly clear sign of Jesus' poverty, understood as freedom from himself, from things, and from other persons, is his choice of virginity. This is not born of any disdain for human love or for women, for whom on the contrary Jesus shows great respect. No, the choice Jesus made of virginity was the fruit of a greater self-giving, of the need to belong totally and unconditionally to his mission. Because of this, his celibacy is never a form of escape or the consequence of being in some way personally troubled; it is rather an extraordinary ability to "be all things to all persons," to love each person according to his or her need, in toughness or tenderness, always going to the heart of the person who stands before him, without preconceptions or fear.

Jesus' poverty is never pessimism about, or disdain for, the world and human beings. He loved life intensely, as is demonstrated by the blood he sweated at death's approach; he also loved this earth tenderly, as is evident in the way he talked about the lilies of the field, the birds of the air, and the whole of the world he brings to such pulsating life in his parables. He loved his neighbor without reserve, even those who crucified him, for whom he asked the Father's forgiveness in the dark and terrible hour of the cross (Luke 23:34).

The mystery of Jesus' poverty is thus the mystery of a freely given and total love, which does not hold back when faced with resistance or refusal. This great love of his gave meaning, unity, and strength to his life and filled him with gratitude to his Father, the "Lord of heaven and earth" who hid "these things from the wise and the intelligent" and "revealed them to infants" (Matt. 11:26). Before announcing the beatitudes of the Kingdom in words, Jesus experienced them in his life, incarnating the words he spoke in the choices he made. In this sense, the beatitudes are nothing other than Jesus' own autobiography: "Blessed are you who are poor. . . . Blessed are you who are hungry now. . . . Blessed are you who weep now . . ." (Luke

6:20-21). His poverty, born of the radical choice he made in freedom, fills him with joy and makes him able to experience awe and gratitude for the gift of the Father's ever new fidelity. Poor as regards the past and so open to the future, poor as regards the present and so able to transform it with imagination and courage, Jesus is also poor as regards the future: he perceives its darkness and menace, but he knows how to go out and meet it, overcoming the temptation to be afraid, entrusting himself completely into his Father's hands.

Faced with Jesus' radical freedom and the way he lived, those who want to be his disciples cannot but ask themselves: What about me? Am I as truly free as Jesus asks me to be? What is the fundamental option of my life? Is it God and his Kingdom? Do I seek to please God alone? And so do I live poorly, rich only with the Father's love? And does the church — which we love and want to build ever anew in the power of the Spirit — live poorly, so as to be as much as possible the faithful and transparent image of the Lord Jesus?

We ask for the gift of this freedom, using the words of St. Ignatius of Loyola:

> Eternal Lord of all things, I make my oblation with Thy favour and help, in presence of Thy infinite Goodness and in presence of Thy glorious Mother and of all the Saints of the heavenly Court; that I want and desire, and it is my deliberate determination, if only it be Thy greater service and praise, to imitate Thee in bearing all injuries and all abuse and all poverty of spirit and actual poverty, too, if Thy most Holy Majesty wants to choose and receive me to such life and state. Amen![3]

---

3. St. Ignatius of Loyola, *Spiritual Exercises* 98.

2

Jesus: Situating His Freedom

How did Jesus "situate" his freedom? That is, how did he exercise that freedom in the real, historical situations in which he acted? What position did he take vis-à-vis the political and social world of his time? A brief overview of the historical context of Jesus' earthly life will help us answer these questions.

Jesus was born in the year 7-6 BC, and so at least two years before the death of Herod, which took place in 4 BC. The king ordered the killing of all infants two years old and younger, thus hoping to eliminate the baby sought by the Magi. (It was the monk Dionysius the Small who made the error in computing the date of Jesus' birth, at the time when it was decided to count the years beginning from that event.) Jesus was born under the Emperor Augustus (63 BC–AD 14; cf. Luke 2:1), at Bethlehem in Judea, where his family had gone to register in a census. They came, in fact, from Nazareth in Galilee, a small town named after the *netser* or messianic "shoot," which had been resettled around the middle of the second century BC by a group of messianic Jews, who moved there from Judea at the behest of the Hasmonean Hyrcanus; their purpose was to bring the town, which in the meantime had reverted to paganism, back into the Jewish fold. The insignificance of the place, located to boot in a semi-pagan region, gave it a very bad name among pure Israelites: "Can anything good come out of Nazareth?" asked Nathaniel, whom Jesus called "truly an Israelite in whom there is no deceit" (John 1:46-47). These reasons for the resettlement of the town explain, however, the messianic fervor that fired the small community and the Davidic ancestry of the family into which Jesus was born.

The young Nazarene spoke Galilean Aramaic, but he also knew Hebrew, the language of the Scriptures. He could express himself, too, in Greek and Latin, as is evidenced by his conversations with the Roman centurion and with Caesar's representative in Jerusalem at the time of his trial (a Roman would never have spoken to a Jew except in Greek or Latin!). His putative father, Joseph, a *tsaddiq* or righteous man, was a carpenter, and this also must have been the young Jesus' trade. His relatives expressed their dismay at the beginning of his public life: "His family . . . went out to restrain him," Mark informs us, "for people were saying, 'He has gone out of his mind'" (3:21). The young Galilean acquired his general education in the synagogue school, but he also drew upon the unique experience of his mother, Mary. After being baptized by John, Jesus began his public ministry, first in Galilee, against the backdrop of Lake Tiberias, and then in Judea, at Jerusalem. He was about thirty years old at the time (Luke 3:23). We cannot, however, be certain about how long the period of his preaching lasted, because John speaks of three Passovers (2:13; 6:4; 11:55), while the Synoptics mention only one.

Jesus' earthly existence can be divided into five periods, separated by the times he chose to dedicate to prayer: the years of silence in Nazareth; the Galilean spring; the Galilean crisis; the journey to Jerusalem; and the events of the passion. He was crucified under the procurator Pontius Pilate, probably on April 7 in the year 30. The *titulus crucis,* the stated reason for his condemnation, written on a tablet attached to the upright beam of the cross, describes him as a political agitator: "Jesus of Nazareth king of the Jews." His death bears all the marks of a political-religious assassination, which in various ways involved the Jewish leaders and Pilate. In fact, in Jesus' time, the land of Israel was a country marked by deep divides: alongside the great majority of the people — made up of day laborers, beggars, small craftsmen, fishermen, and traders — were the representatives of official Jewry, who were in cahoots with the Roman occupier, and the revolutionary groups, the religious reform movements, and the members of heretical Jewish sects.

The highest expression of official Jewry was constituted by the Sanhedrin in Jerusalem, which was composed of the representatives of the priests, of the elders of the people, and of the scribes. While the priests formed a stable tribal entity, in the context of which priestly dignity was passed down in a hereditary manner, and to which the worship in the Temple of Jerusalem was entrusted, the elders of the people were the heads of the most influential and financially well-off families. They were opposed to anything that might disturb the status quo; in politics, as in religion, they were strongly conservative, and this made them close to the party of the Sadducees. The scribes, finally, were lay theologians who attained this status by means of a long and punctilious training; they were surrounded by disciples and treated deferentially by all. They constituted the official "intelligentsia" of the Jews and were able to exercise very considerable influence over the people, because the teachers in the synagogues were drawn from their ranks.

When Jesus is brought before the Sanhedrin, he evinces his deep freedom, especially in his final clash with them. While the chief priests, the elders, and the scribes exert themselves to find proofs by which to condemn him (cf. Mark 14:53ff. and parallels), Jesus is not afraid to affirm his messianic identity and to proclaim that the coming of the Kingdom is connected with his person (cf. Matt. 26:64 and parallels). Handed over by the Sanhedrin to the Roman occupier, in the silence of his sovereign freedom, he offers the mystery of his person as his answer to Pilate's question: "What is truth?" (John 18:38). By his freedom the Prisoner confounds the powerful, who cannot but recognize in him the mysterious revelation of the truth about the human person: "Here is the man!" (John 19:5).

If the Sanhedrin was the institution of official Jewry, the Sadducees and Pharisees were its parties. The Sadducees — whose name derived from either that of Zadok, high priest at the time of Solomon, or *tsadduqi*, which means righteous — were the party of the lay and priestly nobility. Concentrated mainly in Jerusalem and less influential than the Pharisees in the rest of the country, they were conservative in politics and religion: preoccupied with defending the privileges of their own class, they distrusted any hint of change, especially in the interpretation of the Law. Rigidly against any suggestion of doctrinal development, they were, among other things, fierce opponents of the "modern" doctrine of the resurrection of the dead (cf. Mark 12:18ff.; Acts 23:8). One can thus readily understand their instinctive initial distrust of, and then their outright opposition to, the Galilean prophet, whom they saw as a layman of obscure origins, who advanced absurd and dangerous claims regarding the traditional faith and established order.

The Pharisees, on the other hand, came from the middle classes: a lay movement, born at the time of the Maccabees in opposition to any compromise with the Hellenistic world (hence their name, which means "separated"), their original aim was to restore the scrupulous observance of the law in its every last detail. This original rigor, which led Paul to recall his own Pharisee origins with pride (cf. Gal. 1:13; Phil. 3:5), over time became exaggerated formalism and enslaving casuistry. Because of this, although Jesus sat at table with them (cf. Luke 7:36ff.; 11:37ff.; 14:1ff.) and — according to Luke (13:31) — was warned by them about Herod's intention of having him arrested, it was inevitable that he would eventually clash with them: he challenged their authority and condemned their hypocrisy (cf., for example, the five controversies recounted in Luke 5:17-26, 30-32, 33-39; 6:1-5; 6:6-11, as well as Jesus' stern denunciations of them in Luke 11:37ff. and Matt. 23). The truth made Jesus free from the prejudices and fears of those who, like the Sadducees and Pharisees, made their choices on the basis of calculation or in defense of party interest.

Alongside, or rather in opposition to, official Jewry were the revolutionary movements, which more or less violently espoused a radically reformist program on worship, the temple, and the priesthood, and who dreamed of liberation from Roman oppression and the restoration of the kingdom of Israel. Among the various groups that existed at the time, the most important were the Sicarii and the Zealots. The former, named after the small dagger they used in sudden attacks on their enemies while mingling with the crowds, came from Galilee and drew their converts from among the working-class and the poorer farmers. The Zealots, in contrast, were drawn from the priestly nobility and lower clergy; concentrated mainly in Jerusalem, their dream was of an Israel organized once again as a theocracy. Their name speaks of the "zeal" with which they pursued this program; firmly intent on establishing the Kingdom of God here and now, they had no hesitation in using violence against the hated occupiers and their supporters, especially the priestly aristocracy. Some of Jesus' disciples were drawn from these revolutionary movements: Simon, in fact called the Zealot (cf. Luke 6:15; Acts 1:13), had certainly been one of them; Judas, the Iscariot, very probably came from the ranks of the Sicarii (cf. Mark 3:19 parallels); and perhaps Peter, the "barjona," came from similar circles (the Barjona were a terrorist group).

Some of Jesus' characteristics appear to indicate that he was close to the revolutionaries of his time: he preached that the coming of the Kingdom was near; he had a deep sense of a mission that would be decisive in ushering that Kingdom in; he made the enigmatic statement that "the kingdom of heaven has suffered violence, and the violent take it by force" (Matt. 11:12 and Luke 16:16); he was critical of Herod and of those who held power (cf. Luke 13:32; 22:25ff.); he exercised influence over the crowds, who wanted to make him king; he purified the temple and made a triumphal entrance into Jerusalem. It is no mere chance that Jesus was condemned as a political agitator and exchanged for Barabbas, who had been implicated in a murder committed during an uprising (cf. Mark 15:7).

Yet the distance between the prophet from Galilee and the revolutionaries of his day is also clear as soon as we consider other aspects of his life and work: his rejection of violence (cf. Matt. 5:39ff.: "But I say to you: Do not resist an evildoer. But if anyone strikes you on the right cheek, turn the other also . . ."; 26:52ff.: "Put your sword back into its place; for all who take the sword will perish by the sword . . ."); his call for the love of enemies (cf. Matt. 5:43-48; Luke 6:27-36); the beatitude concerning the peacemakers (cf. Matt. 5:9); his faithfulness to the law; his friendship with publicans, the hated tax collectors, who worked for the Roman oppressors; the fact that one of them, Levi-Matthew, was even received into the number of his disciples; and his rejection of messianic movements linked to this-worldly politics. All this could not but be a disappointment for the extreme nationalism and violent fanaticism of the Zealots and Sicarii. Jesus does not fulfill the expectations of those who want immediate and violent action to bring about change: in his freedom, he is not afraid to situate himself at another level, refusing to confuse the Kingdom of God that is coming with any one of the possible kingdoms of this world.

Along with this attitude of complete freedom vis-à-vis the revolutionaries, Jesus demonstrates a clear predilection for the poor, the weak, and the marginalized: publicans, sinners, and prostitutes learn what it means to be accepted by him, for he has no hesitation in spending time with them and eating at the same table. In Israel, table fellowship was equivalent to entering into true, living communion with all one's fellow guests. Accepting such table fellowship with sinners and the marginalized, Jesus showed that he was entirely free from the preconceptions that weighed upon the social relationships of his time. Indeed, it is not that he enters into a communion of sin, as was insinuated by the scribes of the Pharisees' party (cf. Mark 2:16), but that sinners, by eating with him, share in a communion of grace: "Those who are well have no need of a physician, but those who are sick; I have come to call not the righteous but sinners" (Mark 2:17).

Nor does Jesus act any differently with the Samaritans, who were despised and marginalized not only because of their impurity contracted from intermarrying with pagans, but also because of their heresy of accepting only the Mosaic Pentateuch as the Word of God and replacing Jerusalem with Mount Gerizim as the supreme place to worship God. Jesus does not avoid their territory, as was customarily the case even at the cost of making long detours in the journey from the north to the Holy City. Indeed, he spends time with them (John 4:20-21) and makes a Samaritan an example of real love (Luke 10:25-37; cf. also 17:16). This gives rise to an accusation against him: "Are we not right in saying that you are a Samaritan and have a demon?" (John 8:48). But his freedom is more than a match for such accusations, and he does not halt before them, continuing to give the very first place in his life to the impelling necessity of proclaiming the Kingdom.

Worthy of special mention in this context is the way Jesus related with women. Among the Jews, women were considered subordinate to men and were expected to serve them as wives and mothers. Both in the temple and in the synagogue, they were confined to a specially delimited area, and they were considered to have the religious duties of slaves, since — like slaves — they were not held to be free to dispose of their own time. Because of this, they were not even given instruction in the law. They had no voice in civil affairs, nor were they considered in any computation of the number of those making up the assembly of the people in civil life (see, for example, the census of Numbers 1:2, which excludes women, as well as the exclusively male rite of circumcision by which access was gained to the chosen people).

When Jesus comes into the picture, he manifests an entirely new attitude to women, which can without exaggeration be termed revolutionary: he welcomes both men and women without distinction, thus affirming their completely equal dignity in the Kingdom that is coming. The way he behaves disconcerts even his disciples; the evangelists Matthew and Mark, for example, are more than tactful regarding this matter and mention only the group of women who followed Jesus to Calvary and at the resurrection. Luke and John seem somewhat freer in this regard: Luke has no hesitation in mentioning the women who followed Jesus (cf. Luke 8:1-3), and he alone tells of the episode where Jesus meets, and forgives, a sinful woman in the house of a Pharisee (cf. Luke 7:36ff.). John straightforwardly recalls how Jesus' behavior surprised his disciples (John 4:27) and gives many examples of the free and liberating way Jesus related with women. To all, women and men without distinction, the Christ of God opens the doors of the new creation.

At the heart of Jesus' predilection for the marginalized, sinners, oppressed, and weak — not excluding children, with whom it was not considered dignified for a rabbi to concern himself, but whom Jesus welcomed with joy (Matt. 19:13-14 and parallels) — there is his unconditional dedication to the cause of the Kingdom and his total love for the Father and for all human persons, which frees him from prejudice and fear. His attitudes are not born of a mere human thirst for justice or of a kind of social reformism, but from obedience to the One who especially loves and welcomes the humble and sinners, because they are better disposed to receive the gift of grace than the proud, blinded as they are by the fascination of power. Jesus shatters all prefabricated schemes. Not allied with the established order, he is also not a political revolutionary. He is not a puritan who disdains earthly realities, nor a severe censor of human behavior, but neither is he one who does not know the desert or the call to penance. Jesus does not let himself be ensnared by any image that might satisfy the expectations of one side or the other; his radical freedom makes him greater than any of the reductionisms within which people would like to constrict him. He is free in the way he proclaims the Kingdom as the freely given and wonderful work of the Father, to which men and women are called to respond by conversion of heart.

Such a revelation of the freedom of the Master summons his disciples to follow him in the same freedom of love. It means that both the community of believers and the individual Christian must be both free and freeing: the following of Christ is a *sequela libertatis,* a following of freedom. For the church to be free in this way means above all for her to live in radical obedience to the Word of God; the church's strength and treasure lie in her unconditional dedication to her Lord. Every other reason to feel safe or to boast would be a blasphemy and a scandal. As disciples of the One who is truly free, Christians will exert every effort to nourish the experience of freedom within themselves and in the world in which they live, by their prayer and their whole lives, without expecting immediate results or the approval of others. Those who are truly free for the Father know how to take account of the unknown; that is, they believe beyond every possibility in the impossible possibility, which the freedom of God, revealed in Christ Jesus, has promised to history. Those who are truly free testify that this freedom, even when it appears to have been defeated, is worth living for and is contagious and liberating, because, like the freedom of Jesus, it is the revelation and gift of a greater mystery. It will be not only by the work of human hands that the world will be freed from the evil that oppresses it; there will be no deep and lasting liberation unless those same hands open themselves in praise and petition to receive the gift that comes from above. The modern approach to human emancipation — understood as a process of liberation effected by worldly power alone — has always produced totalitarian systems and the manipulations of every kind that are typical of ideologies. The only liberation that does not disappoint is that which has been offered to history in Jesus Christ: liberation from self, to live, in love and hope, for the Father and for others. Jesus, the truly free human being, never ceases to challenge women and men to be free.

Called to follow Jesus where he himself goes before us, we sense that we cannot avoid the questions his freedom poses: Am I free in relation to myself? To others? To things? Am I free for God? For others? How do I live out my fundamental option in the choices of each moment of my life? How do I live, how do we live, the preferential option for the poor that Jesus made? We ask him, the truly free human being, our only authentic liberator, to make us free with his own freedom:

Lord Jesus,
you were the truly free human being:
you gave yourself for love of your friends;
    in all things you sought the will of the Father.
Free from yourself, free for the Father and for others,
grant us, we pray, freedom of heart:
not the seeming freedom
of choosing between one thing and another,
but that deeper freedom,
made of hidden sacrifice and self-giving,
born of the unconditional gift of self.
Free with the freedom of love,
we will, O Lord,
in the days of our mortal life,
be free from our own freedom itself,
and, living out our offering of self,
we will already rejoice at the dawn of the Kingdom that is coming.
So we will prepare in this season of the world
for the new feast of freedom,
which you prepare for us in your glory.
Amen!

3

The Father Sets Us Free:
Lectio Divina on Luke 15:11-32

Not only is Jesus the truly free human being, the example and model of freedom, but he also teaches us, by his life even more than by his words, that the truth will set us free (cf. John 8:32); and since he is the truth (cf. John 14:6), it is he who is our liberator. By his Spirit, Jesus gives us his freedom (cf. 2 Cor. 3:17) and makes us able to welcome the God whom he himself has made known to us as the Father of infinite mercy, and who, forgiving us, makes us free and new in love.

In the story Jesus tells in Luke 15:11-32 he shows us his Father's face. This parable is usually called "The Prodigal Son," but it would more properly be entitled "The Merciful Father." The real main character here is not the son — and in any case there are two sons — but the Father, on whom the two sons, each in his own way, converge. There are thus three characters in this story: the father, at center stage, the younger (prodigal) son, and his elder brother.

The Father of Mercy

The father portrayed in this parable can be immediately recognized as the Father of Jesus. We can gather this from the fact that the parable tells of how the son who had been lost "returns home." In biblical Hebrew — a very earthy language which, because it uses a multitude of images, succeeds in saying everything it has to say with just 5,750 words — the idea of conversion is expressed by the word *shuv*, which means "return" (from the verb *shav* = to return): the God whom Jesus has come to proclaim is thus the Father to whose house we are called to return. This is a God who subverts all our human presumptuousness of teaching God how to be God; this is a "different" God. At least six traits of this God of Jesus emerge from the parable.

The first is *humility*: this story's central character is depicted above all as a humble father. Presented with his son's decision to organize his own life independently of, and even in opposition to, his father, the father offers no resistance. He could certainly have done so on the basis of the Torah, which authorizes the father even to stone a rebellious son: "If someone," says the book of Deuteronomy, "has a stubborn and rebellious son who will not obey his father and mother, who does not heed them when they discipline him, then his father and his mother shall take hold of him and bring him out to the elders of his town at the gate of that place. They shall say to the elders of his town: 'This son of ours is stubborn and rebellious. He will not obey us. He is a glutton and a drunkard.' Then all the men of the town shall stone him to death. So you shall purge the evil from your midst; and all Israel will hear, and be afraid" (Deut. 21:18-21).

But this is not how the father in the parable behaves: he lets his son go. He accepts his son's decision with infinite humility. Humility thus becomes the very first characteristic of the God proclaimed by Jesus. In fact, only God can truly be humble, can truly lower himself to the "humus." Only God can make himself little by making room for another "person" to live, inasmuch as he alone already occupies every place. The humility of God is this drawing back of his so that we might live. In order to speak of this paradoxical divine condescension, the Jewish mystics used the expression *zim-zum*, which tells of God's "contraction" to make room for his creature to exist. This powerful image has a profound meaning: God makes room for the dignity of his creatures. It is as if God somehow limited himself in order that we might live in freedom. The God who can do all things does not want to save us against our own will. Thus, as John Tauler would say, "the virtue hidden in God's deepest depths is humility," inasmuch as only God originally makes room for the other in the profound respect that is born of his creative loving. St. Francis, in his *Praises of the Most High God,* has no hesitation in calling out to the Eternal One with the words: "You are humility!"

This humble God, who limits himself in order that his creatures may live in freedom, is also the father who stands by the window in his home, awaiting his son's return. This is clear from verse 20: "While he was still far off, his father saw him and was filled with compassion; he ran and put his arms around him and kissed him." As suggested by the adverb *makran* in the Greek text, indicating distance, the father had been straining his eyes toward the horizon for a long time, in expectation of his son's longed-for return. The father's attitude, which the parable tactfully and delicately allows us to glimpse here, might be called *God's hope,* the second trait of the father. In fact, humility's second name is hope: if humility means making room for the other to live, hope means going out to the other, longing that he or she might truly come to be, in the free and generous response of love. The Christian God is the God of hope, not only in the sense that he is the God of the promise and thus the foundation and guarantee of every human hope, but also in the sense that he is a God who knows how to wait, full of yearning, and to celebrate when his creature comes home at last.

What allows us to speak of God's humility and hope is the attitude that impels the deeply moved father (*esplanchnisthē,* says the Greek text) to run toward the son who returns. This Greek word echoes the Hebrew *rachamim,* which literally means "maternal entrails": it is used to indicate that God loves with a mother's visceral love, not in proportion to the merits of his creature, but simply because that creature exists (compare, for example, the wonderful words of Isa. 49:14-16 or Ps. 131). Thus the father's third trait in the parable is that he loves with *a mother's love,* a love that leads him to respect his son's freedom to the last and to go on loving him in spite of being rejected. God loves as only a mother can, with a love irradiating tenderness and generosity, more faithful than any possible human fidelity. As St. Bernard would say, "God does not love us because we are good and beautiful, but he makes us good and beautiful by loving us."

This father runs toward his son. For Semites, such behavior was scandalous to say the least, because a father was expected always to carry himself in a solemn, almost hieratic fashion. It was the son who should have presented himself to his father and fallen prostrate before him. The opposite was inconceivable. That the father should go to the son — and not simply this, but, as is said here, that he should run toward his son and throw his arms around him — this was unimaginable. The parable thus presents us with a father who has no fear of losing his own dignity, who, indeed, seems willing to run the risk of forfeiting that dignity altogether. This father's authority does not issue from the distance he maintains, but from the burning love he manifests. This fourth characteristic of the father may be called *God's courageous love:* this is the courage to break with seeming safety, so as to experience the only real safety, a love stronger than non-love, and to move toward the other, overcoming the protective distance that our inability to love only too often creates between us.

The fifth trait of Jesus' God emerges from what the father does when the son arrives home: it is the father's *joy.* Everything he does is an evident expression of this joy. The new clothes, the shoes, the ring, the fatted calf — everything speaks of an altogether special celebration. This, indeed, is the celebration organized in heaven for a single sinner who repents rather than for the ninety-nine righteous who do not need to repent. This is the joy of God.

Yet a God who knows how to be happy has first suffered. If there is a new joy in God, there is also a mystery of suffering that comes before it and that issues from compassion, from the Father's motherly love. This brings us to the last characteristic of Jesus' God, revealed in what has so far been said: the mystery of his *suffering.* The father in the parable does not represent a God who does not suffer, a cold, detached spectator of the world's sorrows, but a God capable of suffering for love of each of his creatures. The parable contains a very important affirmation, at verse 24 and again in verse 32, where the reason for this joy and this sorrow is expressed: "This son of mine was dead and is alive again; he was lost and is found." The first reason for the father's sorrow is that the son "was dead"; he had destroyed himself. The second reason — "he was lost" — is related to the fact that the son had distanced himself from his father. Here is a nuance of quite extraordinary beauty: God suffers first of all because his creature suffers. The first place is not given to the sorrow of his heart, but to the sorrow of the other. God suffers with the sorrow of love.

Aristotle's God, the unmoved Mover, pure Act, is incapable of suffering; but this is not the God of the Bible, who suffers because he loves, because he gets involved in the stories of human beings and accepts poverty out of love for his creatures. This is a God who does not stand aloof from human suffering, imprisoned in divine selfishness, but who knows how to share in humankind's story. There is a mystery of suffering in God the Trinity, which is the other name for God's love for human beings: an active suffering, free with the generosity of love; not a passive sorrow, undergone because there is no way of avoiding it. All the characteristics of the father that the parable allows us to glimpse reveal the mystery of this suffering of love, hidden in the depths of the heart of the Father, the God of Jesus.

The Two Sons: Sharing the Experience of Mercy

Before this father stand his two sons. The younger wants to organize his life entirely on his own. In what does the sin of this son consist? "'Father, give me the share of the property that will belong to me.' So his father divided his property between them" (Luke 15:12). The word "property" here renders the Greek *ton bion,* meaning life and whatever is needed to live. Its use means that the prodigal son does not want his father to have anything further to do with the way he organizes his life. The prodigal son's sin, which is an image of every sin, is a sin of possessiveness, of wanting to be the sole master of one's life, of wanting to put oneself in God's place so as to be completely autonomous.

What destiny awaits this young man? He "traveled to a distant country, and there he squandered his property in dissolute living" (v. 13). Here the Greek verbs, adverbs, and adjectives well express his separation and distance from his father, the waste of property and its painful consequences. Verse 16 gives the clearest expression to the miserable condition into which the younger son descends. Read against the Semitic background, it is truly shocking. In that context, eating together meant a shared life. Since in that same culture the pig was considered the most impure of all animals, a symbol of evil and alienation, when the prodigal son admits that he would gladly eat the pods that the pigs are eating he shows the depths of degradation into which he has fallen: he wants to share the life of the pigs and aspires to their circumstances. This powerful image indicates the magnitude of the drama of sin. To organize one's life in a totally autonomous manner means not really to live any more; it means to lose one's grasp on life's meaning, beauty, strength, and essence. At this point, though, the prodigal son comes to his senses, and the outline of the journey that awaits him — and us — from possessiveness to poverty begins to emerge. It is a journey in five stages.

The first stage, the beginning of conversion, is when we become aware of our *outward exile,* that things are not well with us. This implies that our conversion normally begins from selfish motives: things are not well with me, and I want them to be better. Verse 17 is very important: "When he came to himself, he said: 'How many of my father's hired hands have bread enough and to spare, but here I am. . . .'" In the Greek text, the adversative particle *de* ("but") is very expressive: the young man thinks of how miserable his own circumstances are, even in comparison with the hired hands at home. The first stage of our journey home to God is this awareness of this outward exile, the state of alienation into which we have descended; it means recognizing how miserable we really are.

The second stage of the young man's journey home is when he remembers his father's house and the contrast between his own hunger and the bread given in abundance to the hired hands, who, naturally, are not sons. His awareness of his *outward exile* is thus joined to his *memory of home,* where there is bread in plenty, even for those who are no more than mere employees. Here we are led to understand that it is always important to proclaim the good news of mercy, so that no one may be left without the sweet and saving memory of the love once experienced at home.

In the midst of this awareness of how low we have fallen, and of the plenty we have lost, we gradually begin the third stage in the journey of conversion: we become aware of our *inward exile.* Awareness of outward exile is not enough; we have to become aware that the deepest root of evil is separation from God. "Father, I have sinned against heaven and before you; I am no longer worthy to be called your son" (vv. 18-19). We are separated from the one who loves us immensely. We have wanted to organize our lives in total independence, and so we have become full of self but empty of

God; thus, in the end, we have lost our very selves. This stage of conversion means remembering that we have lost our home through our own fault.

Now comes the fourth stage: the awareness of our inward exile becomes *our no to the past and our yes to God's future for us.* We think again of the home where love awaits us, and we remember that in our father's house there is bread in plenty, because our father is good. Without this fourth stage, conversion would be fruitless. After we have become aware of our outward exile and remembered home, and felt the pain of our inward exile, we have to have hope and believe that a new life is possible. Remembering the home where love awaits us means saying yes to the future, in the certainty that the Father is able to let us begin again from the beginning, in what for us are new and unimaginable ways.

And finally there is the journey's fifth stage: *we really go to the Father.* Everything said so far about the four previous stages must now be translated into action; we must really go to the house of God. This is what makes our change of heart visible: "I will get up and go to my father" (v. 18). This is the decision without which conversion is nothing more than a pious desire, not translated into the new life that transforms a person's destiny. We can never insist enough on the importance of going frequently and faithfully to the sacrament of forgiveness, where the encounter with the minister of reconciliation signifies our return to God and our being welcomed back by the mercy of the Father. From possessiveness the young man has made his way to poverty: this is the journey of his freedom. From being apparently free from the father to live for himself out of his own possessions, now he is free from himself to live for his father, totally and unconditionally open to God in poverty of heart and life.

Finally, there is the other son, the third and last character in the story, the firstborn who has never left home and so has always been physically close to his father; he has, we might say, never left "the courts of the house of the Lord." And yet from the way he behaves it becomes immediately clear that outward proximity does not necessarily mean nearness of heart. One can live the whole of one's life in God's house and yet not love God. It is not enough to rely on being inside the walls of the house of the Lord. What really matters is being close to God's heart, deeply in love with him.

So what happens to this elder son? He has lived out his own story. As he returns home from work he hears the music, wonders what is going on, seeks information, becomes angry, and refuses to go into the house: in other words, he cannot forgive his father for having forgiven his brother. The sin we meet here is the very same sin committed by the younger son. The elder son wants to organize his own life entirely on his own, to be the sole arbiter and judge of what is good and evil, no more and no less than his prodigal brother. Even though we stay near the Father's side, we can also be so far from him as to imagine that we are able to judge the life and heart of others.

And what of the father? How does the central character in Jesus' story respond? He comes out of the house to persuade his elder son, almost as if to ask forgiveness for the way he loves the prodigal son. The elder son says some things that are certainly true (cf. vv. 29-30). All the same, the father, faced with his judgmental attitude, calls him to conversion, to leave behind the logic of merit and profit and to move into the logic of love. "We had to celebrate and rejoice, because this brother of yours was dead and has come to life; he was lost and has been found" (v. 32). The father calls the elder son, too, to be converted to poverty, to leave behind the possessiveness of those who imagine they can judge everything and everybody, and to accept the poverty of those who allow themselves to be led by God and judged by him.

The elder son helps us understand how important it is for us to have someone in our lives who tells us the truth about ourselves. When we lose our sense of the meaning and beauty of God as our judge, we are forgetting our need for someone who can tell us, as only God can, who we really are. We all need someone to help us understand who we really are; and the only one who can do this is God our judge — not a human being. The elder son stands for those who think they do not need God as their judge because they are able to judge themselves; they usurp God's work. The Father, instead, calls us to move into the logic of generosity, not judging with the scales of right or wrong, but letting everything weigh on the side of the greater love.

At this point we are left with the problem of knowing what happens next, because the parable does not give us the end of the story. Here perhaps we can offer a suggestion. Probably the parable ends where it does because it must continue in the life of each one of us: we have to be a living *sequentia sancti Evangelii*, a continuation of the holy Gospel, which tells the part of the story left unfinished by the parable. What will be the life of those who are converted from possessiveness to poverty and who unconditionally give God first place in the way they live? What will be the future of those who experience such a conversion? And what happens, instead, if such conversion is refused or avoided? We must each seek to respond to these questions in terms of our own lives, so as to ask with humility and confidence: In which of the two sons do I discover myself most? In which stage of their journey? In which of their attitudes?

A prayer written by Charles de Foucauld can help us to find our proper place before the God of Jesus, the God who is above all the Father of mercy:

> My Father,
> I abandon myself to you.
> Do with me what you please.
> Whatever you do with me, I thank you.
> I am ready for everything, I accept everything,
> So that your will may be done in me
> And in all your creatures:
> I desire nothing else, my God.
> I entrust my soul into your hands,
> I give it to you, my God,
> With all the love in my heart,
> Because I love you
> And because this love makes me want
> To give myself to you
> And to place myself in your hands
> Without condition,
> With limitless confidence,
> Because you are my Father. Amen.

4

Mary, Listening Lady:
Lectio Divina on Luke 1:26-38

The brightest image of what it means to be a creature who is free for God and for others is Mary, the mother of Jesus, the Virgin who listens. We are helped in understanding this by Luke's account of the annunciation (1:26-38). Luke bases his account on a deeply meaningful biblical model; indeed, he adheres to the same model in his account of the annunciation to Zechariah, the father of John the Baptist (cf. Luke 1:11-20; we thus have what has been called a "diptych of annunciations"). The scheme Luke uses, frequently employed in the Old Testament (for example, in the story of Moses in Exod. 3), falls into five parts: the appearance of an angel; the response of the person addressed; the annunciation itself; the objection(s) raised; the offer of a sign. We can compare these five elements as they appear in the accounts of the annunciation to Mary and to Zechariah; from such a comparison there clearly emerges the message Luke wanted to pass on to his readers.

The first common feature of the two accounts is the *apparition of an angel* to the Baptist's father and to the Virgin Mary. While the angel appears to Zechariah in the temple at Jerusalem (cf. Luke 1:11), the most sacred of all places, he instead appears to Mary in "a town in Galilee called Nazareth" (Luke 1:26), a tiny settlement in a region held in general contempt (as we may readily gather from Nathaniel's question in John 1:46: "Can anything good come out of Nazareth?"). The difference between the two accounts here indicates that the temple's time as the special place of God's presence has now come to an end, and that God instead now makes himself present in a poor and very ordinary place, to a poor, young Galilean woman. The comparison thus underlines that we are witnessing a decisive turning point: salvation is now being offered in a new way, beginning from what the world despises and considers lowly and humble. In this way, Luke gives clear expression to the absolutely generous and unmerited nature of God's initiative, and to the fact that for human beings humility is the first and foremost of the ways that lead to God.

The second element of the two accounts, *the response of the person addressed*, indicates a further difference. As presented by Luke, Zechariah and Elizabeth are "righteous before God, living blamelessly according to all the commandments and regulations of the Lord" (Luke 1:6). Devotedly observant of the law, the couple represents the highest human fulfillment of God's laws, and thus the best that creatures can humanly be in the presence of their Creator. Who, then, is Mary? The word used in verse 28 — *kecharitōmenē* — is difficult to translate: it is the perfect passive participle of *charitoō*, a causative verb. It means that Mary is entirely under the influence of God's favor, and that is where she remains; that she is filled with God's active, dynamic, and entirely freely given benevolence. Thus, while the observant religiosity of the Old Testament finds fulfillment in the Baptist's parents, what shines out in the Mother of Jesus is the freely given and powerful initiative of God. What will happen in Mary will not be the fruit of flesh and blood, because she has found favor with God. Mary is the silence in which the word of the Eternal One is spoken; she is the place of the advent of pure grace. And yet, precisely thus, she is really free, free with a freedom that is given her, which is the very "impossible possibility" granted by God's grace.

The third feature of the account is the *annunciation by the angel*, expressed especially in the invitation, "Do not be afraid," extended both to Mary and to Zechariah (Luke 1:13, 30). The content of the message is, however, different in the two cases. The angel tells Zechariah that the son he has longed for will be born: he is promised the fulfillment of his human longings. To Mary, instead, the angel says: "You have found favor with God. And now, you will conceive in your womb and bear a son. . . . He will be great, and will be called the Son of the Most High" (vv. 30-32). What comes to pass in Mary is God's absolutely surprising and unprecedented initiative. The God who reveals himself here does not merely respond to the longings of our hearts, but above all he subverts our expectations: this is the price we pay so that he may become the fulfillment of our longings, desires, and expectations at a higher level.

The fourth element is the *objection raised.* Zechariah objects: "How will I know that this is so?" (strictly speaking, the original Greek *kata ti* means "on the basis of what?"). Zechariah asks for some guarantee, almost some proof, of what is promised him: his question reveals a lack of faith. He is not able to trust God's promise. What, instead, happens in Mary? She says: "How can this be, since I am a virgin?" (v. 34: "how" in Greek is *pōs*). Mary asks for no guarantee or sign: she questions God's mystery not because she doubts it, but so that she may be shown the path that, in the obedience of faith, she must travel and indeed desires to travel. The Virgin expresses and confirms this availability of hers in the final words of our passage: "Here am I, the servant of the Lord; let it be with me according to your word" (v. 38). Mary is free from herself, and so able to entrust herself totally to God.

The final feature of the two accounts is *the sign,* the birth of the two babies. On the one hand there is John, "even before his birth . . . filled with the Holy Spirit" (Luke 1:15b), who will prepare the way of the Lord (cf. v. 16); on the other, there is Jesus, who is not only "full of the Holy Spirit" (Luke 4:1) but conceived by the Spirit's power. He will be called the Son of the Most High (Luke 1:32). In him the world's new beginning comes to pass. An interesting use is made here of the verbs. While Elizabeth is said to "bear" or "generate" (in 1:13 and 57 the verb is *gennaō*), Mary "gives birth" (in 1:31 and 2:7 the verb is *tiktō*). This careful use of different terms further confirms the message that the evangelist intends to express in his account of the virginal conception of Mary: what has come to pass in her has happened by the power of the Holy Spirit and is thus not the fruit of flesh and blood, but only of God's free initiative, to which Mary responds with the free assent of faith.

This reading is confirmed by two further elements. The first is the verb used to describe the action of the Holy Spirit in Mary ("the Holy Spirit will come upon you," v. 35) is *episkiazein,* the same employed in the Greek translation of Exodus 40:34-35 to indicate the glory that covers and fills the tent of meeting. Mary is God's dwelling place, the new tent of the covenant, and the One who has come to make his abode in her by the free initiative of the Most High is the equivalent, in an absolutely new and surprising way, of the divine presence that dwelt in the tent of the Old Testament.

The other element is the *Xaire* with which the angel greets Mary (v. 28). Normally translated as "Hail, Mary" or "Ave, Maria," this expression is found in the Septuagint, especially in some prophetic texts, outstanding among which is Zephaniah 3:14: "Sing aloud, O daughter Zion" (cf. also Joel 2:21-23 and Zech. 9:9). It is the proclamation of messianic joy, founded in the fact that God is keeping his promises. God has come to fulfill Israel's expectations in a surprising, unheard of, awesome, and wonderful way. What happens in Mary is the world's new beginning. While in the Baptist's father the observance of the Torah and the expectant longing of God's people reach their peak, in the Daughter of Zion there shines out the primacy of divine grace, the free and generous initiative of divine love, to which she responds by freely entrusting herself to the limitless plans of the Lord.

Thus what strikes us most about Mary in the annunciation is her *faith*, which she expresses in her free, docile, and fruitful assent to grace. Throughout her whole life's journey she makes a gift of her freedom and perseveres in abandoning herself to the living God, willingly letting him lead her into obedience to his Word. The whole of Mary is for God, and from him; in all things she is the place where his Kingdom may come. Mary shows us that faith means letting God love us, letting him work in us and mould us. To live this faith is the very opposite of running one's life in total independence, making one's own plans and wanting to carry them out by one's own strength alone. Faith comes from above, from the other, who is God.

In this sense, Mary conceived in her heart before she conceived in her womb: her greatness lies in the faith by which she consented to trust God in his mystery. She is truly the *Virgo fidelis*, the Virgin who believes, the woman who listens, the place where the Word of God comes, the silence in which that Word can sound out for us. And precisely because of all this, Mary is the Daughter of Zion. In her the Jewish spirituality of the *Shema* finds its highest expression: the way she listens is at one and the same time a confession that God is one alone and a decision to place her life with docility before the Eternal One. This is how she exercises the freedom granted her as a creature, focusing her life on the God of the covenant, who first has focused his life on us.

Thus, when Mary says "Here am I," we can recognize in her, in a singular and eminent way, the fundamental attitudes required of any believer. First of all is the value of *virginity,* not only of the body, but also of the heart — that is, that innocence which means being deeply receptive to the way God is at work in us gifting us with our very own being. This is a radical humility, which makes us totally docile to the lordship of the Eternal One in us.

When Mary says, "Here am I," her *poverty,* too, is an example for the church: she lets go of every possible human safety, of every guarantee somehow linked to human capability and power. When Mary says, "I am a virgin," her words are not born of disdain or fear, of pride or self-sufficiency, but rather of her total self-abandonment to God. Taught by Mary, the church will learn to trust God entirely, not to reject what is human, but rather to reject any compromise with that all-too-human presumptuousness that tries to make itself the sole arbiter of its own destiny. When Mary says, "Here am I," she calls the church to an attitude of critical vigilance toward all those forms of "worldliness" that can insinuate themselves into our hearts, a vigilance required especially of those who have freely chosen to serve God with an undivided heart and to make their very lives a celebration of the primacy of grace alone.

Finally, when Mary says, "Here am I," she is a model for the church inasmuch as she witnesses to her deep experience of *obedience* to God: for Mary, being obedient means dwelling uninterruptedly in God's presence and responding to his will in all its surprise and unexpectedness. Taught by Mary, the whole church and each of the church's baptized members learn to love the inner silence and deep listening where the Word comes to pitch his tent among us, often subverting our own calculations and expectations. This faith, which stands fast under the absolute primacy of God, is anything but mere passivity; when Mary said, "Here am I," she truly "cooperated" in the story of the world's new beginning. By the grace that she

welcomed in freedom, she shared in the yes pronounced by the one medi-
ator between God and humankind, her Son, Jesus Christ (cf. 1 Tim. 2:5). In
Mary, God does not compete with the human race, nor does he raise a
monument to his glory over the ashes of his creatures: the obedient and
freely given cooperation of the Virgin Mary, moulded by grace and welcoming its mystery, is an image of our more general opportunity as human beings, free before our God.

Thus it is that, taught by Mary, the listening lady, we learn how to have
faith, to trust totally in the only One in whom it is right and necessary so
to trust — God himself. To her our hearts turn in contemplation so that
the freedom she received and embraced as a gift may also be ours; and we
do this in the words of Dante, at the beginning of the last canto of his
Paradiso:

> Maiden, yet a Mother,
> Daughter of thy Son,
> High beyond all other —
> Lowlier is none;
> Thou the consummation
> Planned by God's decree,
> When our lost creation
> Nobler rose in thee!
>
> Thus his place prepared,
> He who all things made
> 'Mid his creatures tarried,
> In thy bosom laid;
> There his love he nourished, —
> Warmth that gave increase
> To the Root whence flourished
> Our eternal peace.
>
> Nor alone thou hearest
> When thy name we hail;
> Often thou art nearest

When our voices fail;
Mirrored in thy fashion
All creation's good,
Mercy, might, compassion
Grace thy womanhood.

Lady, lest our vision
Striving heavenward, fail,
Still let thy petition
With thy Son prevail,
Unto whom all merit,
Power and majesty,
With the Holy Spirit
And the Father be.[4]

4. Dante Alighieri, *The Divine Comedy: Paradise,* canto 33 (trans. R. A. Knox).

Second Day

JOURNEYING
TOWARD THE CROSS

Today we will be walking behind Christ, the light of life, as he himself journeys toward the cross, where God speaks in silence and lights up the darkness of our hearts athirst for him. This is the day of the "illuminative way," aimed at conforming our hearts and lives to the crucified Lord (*reformata conformare,* as traditional spirituality has it).

We begin by calling on Jesus Crucified in the words of an ancient prayer:

Jesus Crucified!
I always carry you with me,
I love you above all other things.

When I fall, you raise me up.
When I weep, you bring me comfort.
When I suffer, you heal me.
When I call on you, you answer me.

You are the light enlightening me,
the sun warming me,
the food nourishing me,
the spring-water slaking my thirst,
the sweetness filling my senses,

47

the balm restoring me,
the beauty enchanting me.

Jesus Crucified!
Be my defense in life,
and my comfort and confidence
in my last agony.
And rest your head on my heart
At my last hour.
Amen! Alleluia![1]

1. Medieval French prayer, author unknown.

5

Jesus, the Gospel of Sorrows

The issue of suffering is a challenge for each one of us; indeed, history seems to be made of sorrow, as different interests, classes, individuals, and peoples clash in conflict. Human history could even be called the "history of the world's sufferings." From the very depths of all that is unjust wells up the anguished question about the meaning of all this, as well as a longing for justice. The absence of this justice and our yearning for it hurt most when we come to suffer. This is the problem of God. If there is a just God, why does evil exist? (*Si Deus iustus, unde malum?*) And if evil exists, how can there be a just God? The protest raised by tragic atheism and the resignation that throws in the towel are only seeming solutions, because all they in fact do is seek to eliminate one of the two terms of the dilemma.

The Christian gospel, instead, in its reading of the sorrow that is in God and the God who is in sorrow, begins from the cross of his Son. How? What meaning does Good Friday have for the history of the world? What experience of suffering did the Son of God who came in the flesh really have? How are we to answer these questions? With the discretion and tact required of us in the presence of every experience of finitude, and all the more necessary in the presence of Jesus' own experience, we need to draw near to him as he journeys to the cross and to the dark hour of his death; we need to draw near to all that these things reveal about the mystery of God and the salvation of humankind. This is the gospel of sorrows.

It may be said that the whole of Jesus' life was directed toward the

49

cross: the Gospel narratives themselves are sometimes described as "accounts of the passion, with a detailed introduction" (Martin Kähler). The "days of his flesh" (cf. Heb. 5:7) are passed without exception under the grave and sorrowful sign of the cross: "the whole of Christ's life was cross and martyrdom."[1] It was in this sense that the early Christian community spoke of Christ as the "man of sorrows" described first by the prophet (cf. Isa. 53:3): "Like a sheep he was led to the slaughter, and like a lamb silent before its shearer, so he does not open his mouth. In his humiliation justice was denied him . . ." (Acts 8:32-33). Jesus is the Servant, the Innocent One, who suffers out of pure love under the weight of the world's injustice.

Is such a reading of the works and days of Jesus of Nazareth justified? The Gospels are very discreet about this; the testimony they offer is neither emotive nor sentimental. It nevertheless allows us to glimpse, in the things that happened to the Son of Man, at least three levels of the human experience of suffering: physical, psychological, and moral or spiritual suffering.

The Gospels do nothing to conceal the very human aspects of Jesus' *physical limitedness:* his hunger (cf. Matt. 4:2 and Luke 4:2: "he was famished"), his thirst (cf. John 19:28: "I am thirsty"), his sleep (cf. Mark 4:38 and parallels: "he was in the stern, asleep on the cushion"). The cry of the dying Jesus (cf. Mark 15:34) is, among other things, a sign of searing suffering on the physical level. At first sight, these points might seem marginal, but in fact they are not: against every attempt to "safeguard" the divinity of the Son by diminishing the substance of his humanity, from the very beginning the church sought forcefully to insist upon the truth of the incarnation, by which our own, human flesh is offered and promised salvation in the flesh of the Redeemer of humankind.

It is no accident that over the centuries great mystics and saints have focused on the physicality of Jesus, in all the truth of his limitedness: there is, for example, their loving veneration of the Lord's wounds, so passionately venerated by St. Francis that he received them in his own flesh; there are the prayers of St. Ignatius ("Body of Christ, save me. Blood of Christ, inebriate me. Water from the side of Christ, wash me . . ."); and there is the

---

1. Thomas à Kempis, *The Imitation of Christ* 1.2.12.

tenderness for the newborn baby Jesus in the songs composed by St. Alphonsus de Liguori. Truly, Christianity is not a religion of salvation *from* history, but salvation *of* history: no disincarnate spirituality can be justified for the disciples of Christ, whom the Early Middle Ages loved to call "Dominus humanissimus."

The tact of the Gospels is even greater in the silence surrounding the *inward limitedness* experienced by Jesus; they break that silence only with unexpected hints and echoes that reveal his familiarity with the limitations of the human condition and with suffering itself. Thus emerge some aspects of the experience he had of psychological finitude: Jesus grows "in wisdom and in years, and in divine and human favor" (Luke 2:52). In his human awareness of being the Son, he thus moved from a present, implicit level to an ever more explicit level. This "putting into brackets" of his divine awareness is just one aspect of the more general "kenosis" toward which he allowed his love for humankind to impel him (cf. Phil. 2:6ff.). It also explains how, as he journeyed in self-awareness as a man, there were shadow zones when he constantly felt the need of reaching for the light and comfort of his ongoing conversation with the Father in prayer. The heaviness he felt when faced with the suffering and death that awaited him can be glimpsed in what Origen called with loving tact the *"ignorantia Christi"*: thus Jesus showed that he did not know the day of judgment (cf. Mark 13:32 and Matt. 24:36), and in Gethsemane he prayed that he might be spared the chalice of the passion (cf. Luke 22:42). His soul was "troubled" (John 12:27): "in his anguish he prayed more earnestly, and his sweat became like great drops of blood falling down on the ground" (Luke 22:44), even though his heart was entirely handed over to the Father in prayer.

Thus the man Jesus — no differently from every other human being — grew in the school of suffering, as the author of the letter to the Hebrews assures us: "In the days of his flesh, Jesus offered up prayers and supplications, with loud cries and tears, to the one who was able to save him from death, and he was heard because of his reverent submission. Although he was a Son, he learned obedience through what he suffered" (5:7-8). All this certainly takes nothing away from the extraordinary and prophetic awareness with which he so frequently appears to be endowed (thus for example in John 6:71 and 13:11, with reference to his betrayal by

Judas, or in Mark 2:6-8, in relation to the hidden thoughts of the scribes). Yet, in the very human traits of a certain psychological limitedness, there is a special revelation of how Christ truly shared in our human condition, of how he is truly our companion in the pain we so often experience at the times of our own darkness, or when we are brought face to face with the mystery of suffering in others. It is precisely because he has known this condition that he can come to our aid as "the source of eternal salvation for all who obey him" (Heb. 5:9).

Finally, Jesus knows what it is to experience suffering on the *moral and spiritual level:* faced with the death of his friend, he did not hold back his tears (cf. John 11:35), showing that he feels the pain that only love knows: "See how he loved him!" (11:36). At the thought that his last hour was approaching, his soul was "deeply grieved, even to death" (Mark 14:34), with a sadness that reveals how attached he was to life, which has been, and still is, the comfort of countless moments of our own human sadness (we need only think of St. Thomas More, who while awaiting an unjust death found strength in writing his *De tristitia animae Christi*).

When heard against the quiet of the Gospels' usual discretion, Jesus' loud cry from the cross becomes even more searing: "My God, my God, why have you forsaken me?" (Mark 15:34). Do these words point to the depths of an infinite sorrow? Jesus, in reality, has stood at the mysterious and bitter threshold of death, and this inner experience of finitude means that he truly understands human suffering. His compassion for the crowd (cf., for example, Matt. 9:36; 15:32) and the way he was moved by the unfortunate and suffering (cf. Mark 1:41; Matt. 20:34; Luke 7:13; etc.) reveal a sensitivity to other people's pain that only those who themselves have experienced pain can have. The Suffering One, who understands and loves, offers refreshment and strength to whoever is weighed down by suffering: "Come to me, all you that are weary and are carrying heavy burdens, and I will give you rest. Take my yoke upon you, and learn from me; for I am gentle and humble in heart, and you will find rest for your souls. For my yoke is easy, and my burden is light" (Matt. 11:28-30).

To this experience of inner limitation and to the compassion for the suffering of others that derives from it is added in the life of Jesus the very deep impact of the pain inflicted on him by human beings: considered in-

52

sane by his relatives ("He has gone out of his mind": Mark 3:21), accused by the scribes of being possessed (cf. Mark 3:22 and parallels), dismissed as an impostor by the powerful (cf. Matt. 27:63), he felt the whole weight of the hostility accumulating against him. He was saddened not by the accusations but by the hardness of heart from which they issued (cf. Mark 3:5). His adversaries never tired of attacking him in every possible way: his unheard-of claims irritated them (cf. Mark 6:2-3; 11:27-28; John 7:15; etc.), and his popularity frightened them (cf. Mark 11:18; John 11:48; etc.). Jesus undermined their certainties, and, with his success among the people, threatened to shake the precarious *status quo* to its very foundations. However, Jesus was too free to draw back before their threats, and so he continued along his road, faithful to the radical yes he had said to the Father. He became, it is true, more careful, managing to flee from attempts to stone and arrest him (cf. Luke 4:30; John 8:59; 10:39); he avoided confrontation (Mark 7:24; 8:13; etc.). Jesus was no romantic hero, hotheaded and heedless of danger. But in this crucible of suffering, he knew and brought into sharper focus the choice that marked the turning point of his last days on earth: the decisive journey to Jerusalem, the fulfillment of his vocation. "The city of the great King" (Matt. 5:35) is the place where the destinies of Israel and of her prophets must be accomplished (cf. Luke 13:33).

With Jesus' entry into Jerusalem the story of his passion begins in earnest. Jesus headed there with determination (cf. Luke 9:51: literally "he set his face like flint toward Jerusalem"), walking ahead of his own, who followed him disconcerted (cf. Mark 10:32). In David's city, the conflict reached its apex: the Sanhedrin were deeply involved now, as were both the lay and priestly aristocracies that that body represented. Jesus was aware of the iniquity that was about to play itself out in his regard, but he confronted it with the wealth of understanding of one who sees in a death unjustly inflicted his own free self-giving, lived in obedience to the Father, a death that therefore brings life. Proof of this are the accounts of the Last Supper, when the Servant entrusted to his own the memorial of the new covenant in his blood.

In the context of this limitedness, the source of the suffering that Jesus freely accepted, is to be situated the story of his trial: this was the hour of his enemies, "the power of darkness" (Luke 22:53). Why was Jesus condemned? In the eyes of the Sanhedrin he was a blasphemer (cf. Mark 14:53-65 and parallels), one who with his words and deeds (above all the "scandalous" cleansing of the temple: cf. Mark 11:15-18 and parallels) had merited death according to the Law (cf. Deut. 17:12). And yet Jesus was not subjected to the punishment reserved for blasphemers, which was stoning (cf. Lev. 24:14); he was punished by the Roman occupiers, receiving the sentence inflicted on slaves who deserted and on those who subverted the Empire, the ignominious death on the cross. His sentence was a political one, as is witnessed by the *titulus crucis,* the inscription with the cause of his condemnation, placed on the wood of shame: "Jesus of Nazareth, the King of the Jews" (John 19:19). In the eyes of the law his death was the death of a blasphemer, and in the eyes of the powerful, the death of one who sought to subvert the status quo. Easter faith recognizes this day, instead, as the day when, in the Innocent One who died, the Son of God gave himself up to death for us.

As we meditate on this "gospel of sorrows," we cannot but ask ourselves how we live our daily experience of limitation and our inevitable encounter with the suffering in our own lives and in the lives of others. We know that the disciple is not greater than the Master: if he suffered, how can we avoid the path of suffering? Are we able to say with Paul: "I am now rejoicing in my sufferings for your sake, and in my flesh I am completing what is lacking in Christ's afflictions for the sake of his body, that is, the church" (Col. 1:24)? The fear and trembling of our various possible answers can be overcome with the only certainty that makes it possible to risk everything: the certainty of faith. The Master gives us what he asks of us and never tests us without offering us a way forward; he is with us at the hour of suffering, and he helps us to bear and offer our pain.

Ignatius of Loyola was so deeply convinced of this that he had no hesitation in inviting us to follow Jesus along the way of the Cross by way of three kinds of humility, the third of which is the consummate goal toward which to move in the Savior's company:

> The first manner of Humility . . . namely . . . that in everything I obey the law of God . . . ; the second . . . namely . . . I feel no inclination to have riches rather than poverty, to want honor rather than dishonor, to de-

sire a long rather than a short life . . . ; the third is most perfect Humility, namely . . . in order to imitate and be more actually like Christ our Lord, I want and choose poverty with Christ rather than riches, opprobrium with Christ . . . rather than honors, and I desire to be rated as worthless and a fool for Christ, Who first was held as such, rather than wise and prudent in this world.[2]

If obeying the commandments can be costly, if complete submission to the will of God can cost even more, how costly will it be when we choose to imitate the poor, suffering, and abandoned Christ? And so to him we now turn to ask the help of his grace, saying:

Lord Jesus,
suffering Servant of God,
despised and rejected of men,
man of sorrows,
acquainted with grief,
you who have borne our sins
and carried our sorrows,
innocent Lamb,
led to the slaughter
without opening your mouth,
give us, we pray,
the firm will
to share in your destiny:
allow us, servants with you,
out of love for the Father
and for our fellow men and women,
to know how to give everything,
proclaiming with our lives
in the sign of the cross
the good news of the coming Kingdom.
Amen.

2. St. Ignatius of Loyola, *Spiritual Exercises* 165-67.

6

The Cross as the Story of the Trinity

The *via illuminativa* — proper to this second day of the exercises — now reaches its original source, the place where God speaks in silence and his darkness is brighter than light: the cross of Jesus. As we approach the mystery of the cross, we recall how in Western tradition the Trinity has often been depicted in the image of the Crucified One sustained by the hands of the Father, while the dove of the Spirit separates and unites the abandoned Jesus and the One who has "abandoned" him (see, for example, Masaccio's *Trinity* in the church of Santa Maria Novella in Florence and the motif of the "Throne of Grace" — *Gnadenstuhl* — in the German tradition). This image is the translation into visual terms of the profound theological idea that perceives the cross as the place where the Trinity is revealed to us. That the cross tells of the Trinity was understood very early on by the infant church, as is shown not only by the considerable space dedicated to the accounts of the passion in the first proclamation of the gospel but also by the theological structure underpinning the passion narratives. This structure can be identified in the constant and certainly not accidental recurrence of the verb "to hand over" *(paradidōmi);* charting the various appearances of this verb will allow us to identify two fundamental ways in which Jesus is handed over.

The first has to do with the way the Son of Man is handed over by human beings. His love is betrayed, and he is handed over to his adversaries: "Then Judas Iscariot, who was one of the twelve, went to the chief priests in order to betray him to them" (*hina auton paradoi*: Mark 14:10). In its turn the Sanhedrin, guardian and representative of the law, hands the "blasphemer" over to Caesar's representative: "As soon as it was morning, the chief priests held a consultation with the elders and scribes and the whole council. They bound Jesus, led him away, and handed him over to Pilate" (*paredōkan Pilatō*: Mark 15:1). Pilate, while convinced of the Prisoner's innocence — "What evil has he done?" (v. 14) — yields to the pressure of the mob incited by the leaders (cf. v. 11): "After flogging Jesus, he handed him over to be crucified" (*paredōken ton Iēsoun*: v. 15). Abandoned by all, Jesus is alone in living his exodus from himself till the last. If this were the end, though, his death would be just one more of history's unjust executions, with an innocent person crying out in the face of the world's injustice. The early Christian community knows, instead, that this is *not* the case; that is why this community recounts a second fundamental way in which Jesus is handed over, a mysterious threefold way.

The first of these is when the Son hands over his own self. Paul puts it clearly: "The life I live now in the flesh I live by faith in the Son of God, who loved me and gave himself for me" (*paradontos heauton hyper emou*: Gal. 2:20; cf. Eph. 5:2). The Son hands himself over to his Father for love of us and in our place: "No one has greater love than this, to lay down one's life for one's friends" (John 15:13). Handing himself over like this, the Crucified One takes upon himself the burden of the world's suffering and sin; he journeys to the frontiers of furthest exile from God, so as to make the exile of sinners his own, in the self-offering and reconciliation of Easter. "Christ redeemed us from the curse of the law by becoming a curse for us — for it is written, 'Cursed is everyone who hangs on a tree' — in order that in Christ Jesus the blessing of Abraham might come to the Gentiles, so that we might receive the promise of the Spirit through faith" (Gal. 3:13-14). The cry of the dying Jesus expresses the extreme of suffering and exile, which the Son desired to make his own, so as to journey to the furthest outposts of the world's sorrow, and lead this sorrow to reconciliation with the Father: "My God, my God, why have you forsaken me?" (Mark 15:34; cf. Matt. 27:46).

The second part of this mysterious threefold way is this: in addition to the fact that the Son handed himself over is the fact that the Father, too, handed him over. This emerges from the use of the so-called "divine passive." "The Son of Man is to be betrayed into human hands and they will kill him" (Mark 9:31 and parallels; cf. 10:33-45 and parallels; Mark 14:41-42 = Matt. 26:45b-46). It is not merely human beings, into whose hands Jesus is consigned, that hand him over; neither is it he alone who does this, since the verb here is in the passive. It will be God, his Father, who will hand him over: he "who did not withhold his own Son, but gave him up for all of us" (Rom. 8:32). In the Father's giving up of his own Son for us in this way, he manifests the depths of his love: "God so loved the world that he gave his only Son, so that everyone who believes in him may not perish but may have eternal life" (John 3:16). "In this is love, not that we loved God but that he loved us and sent his Son to be the atoning sacrifice for our sins" (1 John 4:10; cf. Rom. 5:6-11). The cross reveals that "God [the Father] is love" (1 John 4:8-16)!

To the suffering of the Son, there thus corresponds the suffering of the Father: God suffers on the cross as the Father who offers, as the Son who offers himself, and as the Spirit, the love that comes forth from their suffering love. The cross is the story of God the Trinity's love for the world, a love that does not simply bear suffering, but chooses it. While the Greeks and Romans could conceive only of a suffering that is imposed, borne passively, and consequently imperfect, a suffering that thus calls for a theory of divine impassibility, the Christian God reveals a suffering that is active, freely chosen, and perfect with the perfection of love: "No one has greater love than this, to lay down one's life for one's friends" (John 15:13). The God of Jesus is not a stranger to the world's pain, a passive spectator from the heights of his immutable perfection. He is in the deepest sense God-with-us, suffering with all who suffer and coming to our aid by being near us in the cross of his Son. Thus is the heart of God revealed: the Father suffers because he has created us out of love, exposing himself freely to the risk of our freedom, and he loves even sinners in the Only-Begotten One, who made himself one with us. Precisely thus, he is the compassionate God, the Father who suffers with whoever suffers, mysteriously watching over the meaning of human suffering in the depths of his love.

Story of the Son and story of the Father, the cross is no less the story of the Spirit: the supreme act of self-giving is the sacrificial offering of the

Spirit, as John the evangelist perceived: "Then he bowed his head and gave up his spirit" (*paredōken to pneuma:* John 19:30). This is the third part of the mysterious threefold way in which Jesus was handed over. In the hour of the cross, the Crucified One gives up to the Father the very Spirit the Father has first given him, the Spirit he will receive again in fullness on the day of the resurrection. Good Friday, when the Son hands himself over to the Father, and when the Father gives the Son up to death for sinners, is also the day when the Spirit is handed over by the Son to the Father, so that the Son may be abandoned, far from God, in the company of sinners. Just as, for Israel, exile was the time when the Spirit was taken away, so when the crucified Jesus hands the Spirit over to the Father he enters into exile without God; and just as for the prophets the messianic homeland will be the place where the Spirit is poured out on all flesh (cf. Joel 2:28-29), so the pouring out of the Spirit on the Son at Easter (cf. Rom. 1:4) will allow the sinners with whom he has made himself one to enter with him into the communion of eternal life in God. When viewed in the light of this handing over of the Spirit, the cross appears to us in all its radicality as a Trinitarian and saving event: "For our sake he made him to be sin who knew no sin, so that in him we might become the righteousness of God" (2 Cor. 5:21; cf. Rom. 8:3).

Story of the Son, of the Father, and of the Spirit, the cross is the story of God the Trinity. Out of love, the Persons of the Trinity take to themselves the exile of the world subjected to sin, in order that this exile may enter at Easter into the home of Trinitarian communion. Precisely thus we are allowed to catch a glimpse of a mystery of suffering in the depths of the Godhead: as John Paul II writes in his encyclical letter *Dominum et vivificantem*, there is a

> pain, unimaginable and inexpressible, which on account of sin the Book of Genesis . . . seems to glimpse in the "depths of God" and in a certain sense in the very heart of the ineffable Trinity. . . . In the "depths of God" there is a Father's love that, faced with man's sin, in the language of the Bible reacts so deeply as to say: "I am sorry that I have made him." . . . Thus there is a paradoxical mystery of love: in Christ there suffers a God who has been rejected by his own creature . . . but at the same

time, from the depth of this suffering . . . the Spirit draws a new measure of the gift made to man and to creation from the beginning. In the depth of the mystery of the Cross love is at work. (nos. 39 and 41)

God's suffering is no sign of weakness or limitation, nor is it a passive suffering, borne only because it is unavoidable. Speaking of this latter kind of suffering, which bespeaks imperfection and limitedness, Pope Pius X's Catechism affirms that, as God, Jesus could not suffer in this way. In the depths of God, however, there is a different kind of suffering — active, freely accepted out of love for the beloved. Inasmuch as the cross is the story of God the Trinity, it is no blasphemous, atheistic proclamation of a death *of* God, thought necessary so as to make room for human beings imprisoned in their own self-sufficiency; it is, rather, the good news of death *in* God, which means that human beings can now live with the life of the immortal God by sharing in the communion of the Trinity made possible by such a death.

Thus the death *in* God of which we speak here has nothing whatever to do with that death *of* God yelled to the four winds by Nietzsche's "madman"; there does not — nor ever will — exist a temple where the *requies aeterna Deo* can be sung! The Trinitarian love that binds the One who abandons to the One abandoned, and thus binds the Father to the world, will conquer death, notwithstanding death's seeming victory. The fruit of the cross's bitter tree is the joyful good news of Easter: the Comforter of the Crucified One, handed over by the dying Jesus to the Father, is poured out by the Father on the Son in the resurrection, so that the Son in his turn might pour the same Spirit out on all flesh. So the Spirit becomes the Comforter of all the crucified of history, revealing to them that at their side is the strengthening and transforming presence of the Christian God. Jacques Maritain writes: "If people knew . . . that God 'suffers' with us and much more than us from all the evil that devastates the earth, there is no doubt that many things would change, and many souls would find freedom."

The "message about the cross" (1 Cor. 1:18) thus calls us to follow Jesus in a surprising way: it is in weakness, pain, and rejection by the world that we will find God. It is not the splendor of earthly greatness, but the exact opposite, littleness and ignominy, which are the special place of his presence among us, the desert that flowers when he speaks to our hearts. The cross of the living God may now be recognized in the life of every human being: it now becomes possible in suffering to learn openness to the God who is present there, and who offers himself with us and for us, to transform our pain into love, and our suffering into self-giving. The church and every single disciple can thus be understood as the people of the *sequela crucis*, living "under the cross" both as a community and as individuals. Nothing is further from the image of the cross than a community that lives cozy and safe, placing its trust in purely human means: "A settled Christianity where everyone is a Christian, but in inner integrity alone, no more resembles the Church militant than the silence of death resembles the eloquence of the passion" (Søren Kierkegaard).

This church living under the cross is the gathering of those who, with Christ and in his Spirit, seek to leave self behind and to walk the painful way of the cross: "If any want to become my followers, let them deny themselves and take up their cross and follow me. For those who want to save their life will lose it, and those who lose their life for my sake, and for the sake of the gospel, will save it" (Mark 8:34-35 and parallels). "Whoever does not take up the cross and follow me is not worthy of me" (Matt. 10:38 and Luke 14:27). The disciple will have to complete in his flesh "what is lacking in Christ's afflictions for the sake of his body, that is, the church" (Col. 1:24). Compassion toward the Crucified One will thus be translated into solidarity with the members of his crucified body in history. The disciples of Jesus witness to their identity by "losing it," placing it at the service of others to find it again at the only level worthy of the followers of the Crucified One: the level of love. To the disciple, crushed under the weight of the cross or awed by the demands of following the Lord, is addressed the word of promise revealed in the resurrection, the contradiction of all history's crosses: "For, just as the sufferings of Christ are abundant for us, so also our consolation is abundant through Christ" (2 Cor. 1:5). In all those who seek to follow the Master along the *via dolorosa*, the cross of Christ is not emptied of its power (1 Cor. 1:17). In them, too, will be made manifest the victory of the Humble One, who overcame the world (cf. John 16:33).

Jesus Crucified thus questions the way we live: Am I ready to read my life in light of the cross? Am I able to recognize the cross in my life? How do I live out the experience of the cross? In what measure do I help others to carry their cross? The answer we give these questions becomes one with our prayer to the Blessed Trinity, God of the pain of love, who conquers sin and death:

Father, you hand your only Son over for us;
Son, you live the ultimate abandonment of the cross
   and offer yourself to the One who abandons you;
Comforter of suffering,
   you unite the Father who gives and receives
   to the Son who dies,
   and in the Son you unite the Father to the world's passion.
Trinity of suffering,
God hidden in the darkness of Good Friday,
   give us, we pray you,
   the grace to take up day by day
   the cross of abandonment,
   and to offer it with you,
   in ever deeper communion.
There you reveal yourself to us —
   Trinity of love,
   God of solidarity
   and nearness —
to the weakness of your creatures.
Amen.

7

Abraham and the *Aqedah* of Isaac: *Lectio Divina* on Genesis 12 and 22

As we continue this journey in lively remembrance of our Savior, we have the company of that "cloud of witnesses" (Heb. 12:1) whose aid we have invoked from the outset: they have gone before us, fighting the good fight of the faith in an exemplary way. A special place among them is occupied by Abraham, considered the father of believers by Jews, Christians, and Muslims alike. In fact, when Abraham offered his own son out of love for the Eternal God, he introduced into history an absolutely new attitude, one that had never existed until then: faith. Abraham's faith is so radical that the book of Isaiah says: "Look to the rock from which you were hewn, and to the quarry from which you were dug. Look to Abraham, your father" (51:1-2). By his faith, Abraham is like the rock on which our faith rests and from which our spiritual identity takes shape. The apostle Paul, in his turn, has no hesitation in saying that "those who believe are the descendants of Abraham" (*hoi ek pisteōs*: Gal. 3:7), expressing his clear conviction that faith is not produced by our own hearts but is rather a gift we receive from above, just as Abraham did.

Who, then, is Abraham? What was his story, and what was the journey of faith he traveled? The texts to which we look for answers to these questions are above all two, chapters 12 and 22 of the book of Genesis: the call of Abraham and the *aqedah* of Isaac — that is, the episode of the sacrifice on Mount Moriah. We begin our consideration of these texts by asking a preliminary question: What situation is Abraham in when he is called by God? What knowledge of the Eternal One does he have when he sets out on his journey? And when did he truly come to know the Lord?

The rabbinic sources offer us three different answers: some say that Abraham came to know God when he was one year old; others, when he was three; yet others, when he had reached the age of forty-eight. What do these different traditions mean?

In the first tradition, Abraham came to know God at one year old — that is, at an age when we do not yet possess the conceptual or intellectual tools to know him. Thus, according to this tradition, Abraham's knowledge of God was entirely a gift, a grace; everything came from above.

The second tradition affirms that Abraham came to know God when he was three years old. At this age, we already begin to have some understanding of the way things are, and above all we begin to be aware of the influence exercised over us by our family, by those who are bringing us up. In this tradition, Abraham's knowledge of God is the result of two factors: on the one hand, the gift of God, because at only three years a special gift is necessary to come to know God as Abraham did; on the other, some response from Abraham himself and from his family. Here Abraham's knowledge of the Most High would be the fruit of a meeting between the human and the divine, in which his circumstances certainly played their part.

The third tradition is perhaps the most beautiful: Abraham came to know God at forty-eight years of age, and so in full maturity, at the time, as they say, of disenchantment. When we are young, we have many dreams, many plans. Then life brings us up against the bitter experience of disappointment, cuts our dreams down to size, and prunes back our plans; we collide with reality, which is often hard and difficult, perhaps precisely where we would least have expected it. In this third tradition, it was at this very time of life, when we can be much tempted to give in to regret and disappointment, that Abraham, in the absolute poverty of his heart, discovered the absolute primacy of God, certainly not without the gift of light from above. This tradition thus very beautifully underlines two things: on the one hand, the gift of God, and on the other, the fact that we can really discover God only when we have experienced what it means to be a human being, when we have experienced the world's suffering. It is then that we can really understand what the gift of God is: he is no longer a mere human consolation, the refuge of our dreams, the projection of our longings; he is God, and we entrust ourselves to him completely, because we know that no human power, not even the powers in which we had placed such trust, will ever be able to give us truth and peace of heart.

We know from the Bible, however, that Abraham came from a family accustomed to serving other gods: this information is supplied by the book of Joshua (24:2), when it speaks of "your ancestors, Terah and his sons Abraham and Nahor," who "lived beyond the Euphrates." From the point of view of his family background, Abraham thus had nothing that predisposed him to become God's chosen one. His was a family of nomads, and nomads have no security: their roof is the sky, and their future is the surprises each new day brings. Abraham came from a family of idolaters. This complete absence of the human requirements for Abraham to become the father of believers is very significant, because it helps us understand that faith is not simply passed on by heredity; it is not something we can take for granted, but each of us has to attain it by paying the price ourselves, living our own love, suffering our own adventure. Nothing human guarantees or precludes us from the knowledge of God, which is always and only an encounter of grace and freedom.

In any case, according to Genesis 12:4, Abraham's great adventure, his true vocation, begins when he is seventy-five years old; from this we may conclude that it is never too late to begin! Seventy-five years, even at that time, was a considerable age, even if people then tended to lived for a long time, as the stories about the patriarchs suggest. Genesis also informs us that Abraham was a man full of fear; our father in the faith was no hero, but a person with all the apprehensions that we ourselves may at times experience. His story speaks in particular of the fear, so common and deeply rooted in the human heart, of the inexorable onset of death. According to Genesis 12:10-20, when Abraham went to Egypt with his wife Sarah, who was still beautiful despite being well on in years, he invented the story that Sarah was not in fact his wife, but his sister, hoping that if Pharaoh or some other powerful personage in Egypt caught sight of her they would not be tempted to kill Abraham so as to rid themselves of their rival. Abraham was not without guile, and he felt the fears that can affect every human being.

In Abraham, though, there is one special fear, which is at the same time a great sorrow: the thought of dying without an heir. In Abraham's time, faith in personal immortality did not exist; in the common opinion, life was what is lived here in this world, between the first yell of the newborn infant and the last cry of death. Everything a human being might give or receive had thus to be given and received in the years of this mortal life. Abraham could not but be influenced by the mentality of his time; for him it was obvious that the only way to survive death was to have a son. Those who have no offspring die twice: they die at their death, but they die again because there will be no one left behind to pronounce their name with love. So Abraham ardently longs for a son; for him it is a question of life or death. He wants this so much that he lets himself be persuaded to have a child with the slave-girl, Hagar (Gen. 16:1-6): his son Ishmael. In the religious imagination of the East, the relationship between Arabs and Israelis is rooted in this biblical tradition. While the Jews consider themselves the descendants of Isaac, the Arabs hold that they are the descendants of Ishmael; for the Jews Ishmael is only the son of the slave-girl, while for the Arabs he is the son of the promise, since Hagar was just as much a chosen one as Sarah. The effects of Abraham's fears are still with us today.

So, all in all, Abraham is like us, with all the fragility proper to our shared human condition, with all our uncertainties, doubts, and questionings. What happens to this man so as to change his life forever? He encounters God's call. Actually, there are two calls — it is important to distinguish between them — recorded respectively in Genesis 12 and 22. In Genesis 12 the Lord calls Abraham and tells him to leave his country, and his certainties, behind — and this is no easy thing. We must thus take this first call seriously. To leave behind us the things that give us a sense of security is always costly, and it costs even more when we are well on in years, when we have become creatures of habit, more bound to our own certainties, like a dog defending its own little bone. Abraham is no exception. To have to leave Ur of the Chaldeans, his little world made of idols, business, his nomad's life, insecurities, and fears, is no easy thing. We really love our prison!

Yet God promises Abraham something very beautiful, the fullness of blessing, descendants as numerous as the stars in the sky and as the sand on the shore of the sea. To someone without a child a promise like that seems like a dream. And then God promises him the land, and Abraham is a nomad! This is a promise of security and stability forever. It is a promise too beautiful not to accept. So Abraham decides to obey God's voice and set out, leaving his own land and journeying toward the land of God's promise. Yet, in doing this, Abraham is responding to a God who has promised him exactly what he in fact wanted. The call in Genesis 12 is the projection of his heart's desire. In this context even the greatest renunciations — to abandon his own property, his affections, his land — seem bearable, because, as they say, the game is worth the candle.

Yet, if this was all there was, Abraham would not be the father of believers. For faith to exist, it is not enough to have the enthusiasm necessary to follow God when he promises you the things you want. For faith to exist, something more is required, something different, something that deeply transforms your heart, that signs it forever, something that upturns your life and leads you, alone before God alone, to live out the most difficult offering, the greatest gift, the deepest love. This is what happens in Genesis 22:1-18, Abraham's second call, which Jewish tradition calls the *aqedah,* the "binding" of Isaac.

First comes God's command: "Take your son, your only son Isaac, whom you love, and go to the land of Moriah, and offer him there as a burnt offering on one of the mountains that I shall show you" (v. 2). Abraham can find no words; he is silent, and obeys. The God who called him, promising him what he most desired in the depths of his heart, the God who had given him the joy of his Isaac, that same God now asks him to give Isaac up. It is enough to make him lose his mind! How can it be that God himself should deny God's promises? That the same God who made him leave everything to give him everything he desired should now ask him to sacrifice everything — more, to sacrifice the only thing that really matters to him in this life? This is the testing of Abraham. It is the testing of the apparent defeat of God, of a God who seems to betray his own self, who takes from you what he himself has given: how can this be? We can well understand why Abraham finds no words.

One of the finest commentaries on this text is by Søren Kierkegaard in his little book *Fear and Trembling.* When the beloved son, Isaac, asks his father, "The fire and the wood are here, but where is the lamb for a burnt offering?" and Abraham offers him the lapidary reply, "God himself will provide the lamb for a burnt offering, my son" (vv. 7-8), Kierkegaard has Abraham make this secret prayer: "Lord of heaven, . . . it is better that he believes me a monster than that he should lose faith in you."[3] Abraham understands that if he were to tell Isaac that God wants him sacrificed, the boy would no longer be able to believe in God. So he prefers that his son think him a monster than that Isaac lose faith in the Most High. Abraham loves God even to this point: he is not only ready to sacrifice his heart's beloved, but also to be considered a monster by his son rather than allow that son to lose his faith.

Kierkegaard here adds a deeply striking reflection: "Everyone became great in proportion to his *expectancy*. One became great by expecting the possible, another by expecting the eternal; but he who expected the impossible became the greatest of all." Abraham wagers everything on God's impossible possibility, on the fact that the same God who has given and who now takes away is the God in whom we have to trust. God always has something impossible in reserve. Abraham trusts God even when God is silent. In this lies his greatness: trusting God not only when everything goes well, but always, even when he seems to be depriving you of the Isaac of your heart. Kierkegaard goes on: "Abraham left behind his worldly understanding and he took along his faith."[4] Abraham no longer thinks in terms of human calculation: *do ut des*, I give this and I receive the other. Abraham believes, he abandons himself completely to God, he trusts.

Kierkegaard again: "God is the one who demands absolute love." We are not loving God when we love the consolations of God; rather, we love God whenever we love what God plans for us. St. Teresa of Avila, for example, says: God is loved not for his consolations, but simply because he is God. God demands absolute love — and he is the only one who has the right to demand this! As Kierkegaard observes, no sacrifice is too great when it is God who asks for it. And no sacrifice can exclude love. To offer

---

3. Søren Kierkegaard, *Fear and Trembling; Repetition*, trans. Howard V. Hong and Edna H. Hong (Princeton: Princeton University Press, 1983), p. 11.

4. Kierkegaard, *Fear and Trembling*, pp. 16-17.

God the true love of our lives — this is difficult! Abraham "must love Isaac with his whole soul. Since God claims Isaac, he must, if possible, love him even more, and only then can he *sacrifice* him."[5] Abraham can sacrifice Isaac only because he loves him infinitely. We do not offer God our heart's surplus; to God we offer our greatest love. Only if you love infinitely can you offer God the greatest love. So the truth is that we start living by faith when we offer God our heart's beloved, and each of us has an Isaac of the heart. To have faith means to identify this Isaac of ours and be ready to place him on the altar of sacrifice the day God asks for him. To offer the Isaac of our hearts, our only one, our beloved, to God, because only God is worthy of such an offering and must be loved like this — this is faith: to die in order to be born; to lose our life so as to find it.

In Genesis 22, Abraham dies to his dreams and his desires, because he is ready to give God his Isaac, to love God more than all God's consolations, to entrust himself totally to God. Then God can say to him: "Now I know that you fear God" (v. 12), because now Abraham has offered God the Isaac he loves: "Now I know that you fear God, because you have not withheld your son, your only son, from me." How beautiful this is! How demanding! How true, and what a drama it contains! This is faith: to believe in God's impossible possibility, to trust God in spite of everything. Persons who believe trust God even when God appears defeated; they know that God is God and that we must trust him unconditionally. This is why, when the apostle Paul wants to celebrate the love of God by showing how deep it is, he refers back to Genesis 22, without quoting the passage explicitly but using the same words used by the Greek text of the *aqedah* in the Septuagint: "He who did not withhold his own Son, but gave him up for all of us, will he not with him also give us everything else?" (Rom. 8:32). In this kind of application of the biblical text (*midrash*), Abraham becomes the image of God the Father, and Isaac the image of Jesus, the Son — although, while the Isaac in Genesis 22 does not die, the Isaac in Romans 8:32 does, and for love of us. As Origen says: "God competes magnificently in generosity with human beings: Abraham offered God a mortal son who did not die; God handed his immortal Son over to death for hu-

---

5. Kierkegaard, *Fear and Trembling,* pp. 73-74.

mankind."[6] The sacrifice of Isaac thus attains complete fulfillment in Jesus, and Abraham — understood as an image of the heavenly Father who sacrifices his Son — may rightly be considered our father in faith, who knew how to believe against all the evidence and to hope against hope.

Abraham became father in the faith for many peoples, because he loved God more than God's promises, to the point of being ready to sacrifice the Isaac of his heart. Empty of self, rich with God, he would also be enriched with a multitude of children — all those who down the centuries would go on believing that God is faithful even when he seems to have been defeated or silenced. Precisely thus, Abraham challenges us, his children in the faith, to ask: Do I believe in God because he satisfies the desires of my heart, or because God is God? Do I love him for his consolations, or because he is God, my God? Am I ready to offer him the Isaac of my heart on the altar of sacrifice, loving God more than the reward and consolation God may give? Only those who are ready to give God their own Isaac are ready to believe in him and give him their whole lives; we cannot simply offer God a part of ourselves — it is our whole selves that we must offer. Then we will be able to say that we have loved him and that we love him still; then we will be able to live in faith, like Abraham, our father in the faith.

And so we pray:

> Do not let us forget this:
> You speak even when you are silent.
> Grant us this confidence:
> when we await your coming
> You stay silent out of love
> and out of love you speak.
> One and the same thing
> both in speaking and silence.
> You are always the same Father,
> with the same fatherly heart,
> and you guide us with your voice
> and lift us up with your silence.

6. Origen, *Homilia in Genesim* 8.

8

Mary at Cana and at the Foot of the Cross:
Lectio Divina on John 2:1-11 and 19:25-27

Mary, the mother of Jesus, walks with us at every stage in this journey of our retreat. In her life here on earth — as in her Son's — everything points to the cross, beginning from the day when old Simeon foretold that a sword would pierce her soul (cf. Luke 2:35); thus she has no rival as a model and encouragement when we walk our *via illuminativa,* where in the bright darkness of the cross we find the light and strength we need to make our choices of mind and heart. The Gospel of John, characterized by an extraordinary wealth of symbolic language, is of special help in our encounter with Mary, mother and disciple of the Crucified One, for John's Gospel opens and closes with scenes where Mary plays a central role at her Son's side. First, we see her at the marriage at Cana; and second, we see Mary as she stands at the foot of the cross at the supreme moment when the destiny of the abandoned Prophet, the Redeemer of humankind, reaches fulfillment.

John's account of the marriage feast at Cana (2:1-11) has a clear theological purpose, evidenced by verse 11: "Jesus did this, the first of his signs, in Cana of Galilee, and revealed his glory; and his disciples believed in him." Given the importance John attaches to the *sēmeia,* the signs that reveal the mystery accomplished in the Word made flesh, this description of what happened at Cana as their beginning and prototype means that this account is of special significance in the Gospel; we stand before an event that provides the key by which to read the whole revelation of Christ. As a consequence, the attention paid to the mother of Jesus in this passage situates Mary in a position of special importance with respect to the whole mystery of the Redeemer.

Further, the account is introduced by the formula "on the third day" (John 2:1). On the one hand, this recalls the revelation on Sinai: "Prepare for the third day, because on the third day the Lord will come down on Mount Sinai in the sight of all the people" (Exod. 19:11; cf. 19:16). On the other hand, it recalls the resurrection itself: "Destroy this temple, and in three days I will raise it up ... he was speaking of the temple of his body" (John 2:19-21). It is on the third day — in the fullness of time — that God intervenes (cf. Hos. 6:2), in the revelation of his glory on Sinai, at Cana, and in the resurrection; and from these mighty events flows the faith of both the old and new people of God (cf. Exod. 19:9; John 2:11, 22). The marriage feast at Cana is thus an anticipation of the Easter event itself, when the new marriage covenant between God and humankind is sealed, fulfilling and superseding the covenant made at Sinai. Read against the symbolic backdrop of the marriage between the Lord and his people, a most beautiful metaphor for the covenant (cf. Hos. 2:16-25[14-23]; Jer. 2:1-2; 3:1, 6-12; Ezek. 16; Isa. 50:1; 54:4-8; 62:4-5; cf. also the Song of Songs and Psalm 45), the sign given at Cana reveals Jesus as the divine Bridegroom of God's new people, with whom he concludes the new and definitive covenant in his Easter mystery. This is a decisive turning point in the history of salvation, and in it the mother of Jesus has a role, underlined in no chance way by John the evangelist.

It is Mary who notices the problem that has arisen: "They have no wine" (John 2:3). Whether this is a simple statement of fact or whether her words are a request inspired by her confidence that her Son can intervene to help, we see here the tender and down-to-earth concern of Mary the Mother, who presents to her Son their mutual friends' predicament. Wine is mentioned five times in the account (vv. 3, 9, 10), with particular emphasis on the superior quality and abundance of the wine produced by the miracle; this emphasis can be recognized as indicating a sign of the messianic times (cf., for example, Amos 9:13: "the mountains shall drip sweet wine, and all the hills shall flow with it"; according to Isa. 25:6, wine is an important part of the eschatological banquet, where it is offered free; cf.

Isa. 55:1). New wine will bring joy to the day of the eternal marriage between the Lord and his people (cf. Hos. 2:21-24[19-22]; the theme of wine is also frequent in the Song of Songs: 1:2, 4; 4:10; 5:1; etc.). In the light of all this, the marriage feast at Cana can be read as the sign indicating that the promised age has come, the hour of God's intervention at the last times, when he comes to fulfill in an altogether superabundant way the expectations of his chosen people, and to change their water of purification (cf. John 2:6) into the new wine of the Kingdom. The letter of the law is changed into the new wine of the Spirit! In the special place assigned to Mary here, we can recognize in her all Israel's expectant longing and the call, full of yearning, that the first covenant directs to the new.

This interpretation of the marriage feast allows us better to understand Jesus' apparently cutting reply: "Woman, what concern is that to you and to me? My hour has not yet come" (John 2:4). This expression commonly indicates a divergence (cf., for example, Mark 1:24; 5:7; etc.). Here the divergence is between the wine that Mary says is needed and the "new wine" that will be given at Jesus' "hour"; or perhaps — and this would be more in harmony with John's symbolism and his polemic with the synagogue — the divergence is between the expectation of the first covenant, signified by the presence of Mary, and the altogether surprising, new situation that Christ creates and that will be fully manifested at his "hour."

This "hour" is the Easter event of Jesus' passion, death, and resurrection (cf. John 7:30; 8:20; 12:23, 27; 13:1; 17:1; 19:27); the term runs through the Gospel of John to indicate the supreme moment — awaited, announced, and prepared for — of the passage of Jesus from this world to the Father. It is at Christ's hour that the messianic times will be shown to be the fulfillment of the promises as well as the promise of the new and definitive fulfillment. Jesus' reply to Mary thus becomes an invitation to Israel — represented here by the Woman, Daughter of Zion (as is often the case in the Old Testament: cf., for example, Jer. 2:2; Ezek. 16:8; 23:2-4; Hos. 1–3; Isa. 26:17-18; etc.) — to move from the level of the old expectations to that of the new salvation offered in him, the Messiah who has come. Again, the term "woman" with which Jesus refers to his mother could evoke the relationship between her and Eve, equally referred to as "woman" in Genesis 3. The echo of Genesis 1:1 in John 1:1 — "in the beginning" — might thus be the remote background of this parallelism. Jesus the new Adam would thus show Mary to be the new Eve of a regenerated humanity. In this case, there would emerge in even sharper relief the relationship of both continuity and discontinuity between Israel's expectation of redemption and the new salvation represented by the messianic wine offered by Jesus.

The words that Mary addresses to the servants are very important: "Do whatever he tells you" (John 2:5). They recall the making of the covenant at Sinai: as the people of the old covenant responded to the divine revelation with the assent of faith — "Everything that the Lord has spoken we will do" (Exod. 19:8; 24:3, 7) — so Mary manifests her unconditional trust in her Son, who has just evoked the mystery of his "hour." Two things thus become clear: on the one hand, Mary and Israel are being somehow identified, so that she expresses all that is true in the expectation of the chosen people; on the other, her mother's faith is seen to be open to the impossible possibility of the sign that her Son may wish to perform.

Mary's invitation to the "servants" (indicated here by the term *diakonoi*, which John uses in 12:26 to refer to Jesus' true disciples) underlines the role of model and mother in the faith that she will play in the community of the new covenant. In Mary, the old covenant passes into the new, Israel into the church, the law into the gospel, and this by way of her total and unconditional faith in her Son, to whom she directs herself and others: "Do whatever he tells you." In the church born at the Passover of the new and perfect covenant, the Virgin Mother is the one who presents to her Son the needs and expectations of his people and leads them to that faith in him which is the necessary condition for the new wine to fill the jars of the ancient purification. The way to enter the messianic marriage feast — sealed by the blood of the Lamb, offered on the mountain of sacrifice — is faith, to which Mary the mother calls us. She is a living example of this saving, believing obedience: "Do whatever he tells you."

Whatever is prefigured and announced at Cana reaches complete fulfillment in John's portrayal of Jesus' mother at the foot of the cross and in the words addressed by the dying Jesus to her and to the disciple whom he loves (John 19:25-27). The close link between Cana and the cross can be gathered from many elements, including the very presence in both accounts of the "mother of Jesus" (John 2:1 and 19:25), here too referred to as "woman" (2:4 and 19:26), and similar references to the "hour" (John 2:4 and 19:27: "and from that hour . . ."). John 19:28 is also replete with symbolic meaning: "After this, when Jesus knew that all was now finished, he said (in order to fulfill the scripture), 'I am thirsty.'" Jesus the Son's words to his mother and the disciple are thus understood as setting the seal of completion on the task entrusted to him by the Father (cf. John 4:34; 5:36; 17:4). It is as if the Son had to pronounce these words in order for his mission to be entirely fulfilled.

What is the meaning of this densely symbolic passage? Here again, Jesus calls his mother "woman" (John 19:26), a title that evokes the words which the prophet addressed to Jerusalem and the chosen people. As Isaiah would say to Jerusalem: "Lift up your eyes and look around. . . . Your sons shall come from far away" (60:4), so the crucified Messiah says to his mother: "Woman, here is your son." Thus at one and the same time Mary represents the chosen people of the first covenant and the people now gathered together by God through the paschal sacrifice of Christ.

With Jesus' mother stands the beloved disciple (cf. John 19:26). Indicated three times with the definite article — "*the* disciple" (vv. 26-27) — he is further described as "the disciple whom he loved." By employing this kind of emphasis, the evangelist would seem to be saying that this particular disciple stands for *every* disciple who, faithful in love, is especially loved by the Father and the Son. For John, the true disciple is one who is faithful right up to the cross (v. 26) and is thus a witness of the fruitful mystery of the blood and the water that flow from the pierced side of the Crucified One (v. 35), a witness of Jesus' resurrection in a particularly graced way (cf. John 20:8). This is the disciple who at the Last Supper is "in Jesus' bosom" (*en tō kolpō tou Iēsou*: John 13:23, according to the literal translation, which recalls the "maternal entrails," the *rachamim* of the divine mercy in the Old Testament). Beginning at this "hour" of the cross, the disciple takes Jesus' mother "into those things which are most intimately his" (*eis ta idia*: 19:27); this is no mere matter of admitting her "into his own home." For John this expression has to do with a person's life-world, where they really exist (thus, for example, he uses it in 1:11 to speak of Israel in relation to the

Word, or in 10:4, speaking of the disciples' relationship to Jesus). Here it means that Jesus' mother now becomes a vital and inseparable part of the deepest life of the disciple, a treasure of such value as never to be given up again.

So we are now in a position to understand the rich meaning John ascribes to the relationship established by the crucified Jesus between his mother and the disciple. In the first place, Mary the "woman" stands for ancient Israel, and the disciple represents the church that believes: John's conviction is that Israel now becomes a living part of God's new people. In his conversation with the synagogue, the evangelist seems to be saying that the church is the new people of God, that she is not a betrayal but a fulfillment of what has gone before, and, on the other hand, that the church recognizes that Israel is her mother and the door to the very center of the Lord's heart. In the second place, Mary the "woman" here stands for the new people of the messianic times, and the disciple is an image of each individual believer. The fact that they now belong to one another means that "mother church" and the church's sons and daughters also belong to each other; the church is as dear to the disciples as is a beloved mother, a precious treasure entrusted to them by their Redeemer from the cross. Finally, Mary is also that unique, real human being who is the mother of Jesus: here John seems to be underlining the very special relationship between *this* woman and every single believer, as well as between her and the whole family of the Lord. Mary is a precious part of the church and of the disciples' life of faith. In her, the church and individual believers recognize their mother, who has been entrusted to them and to whom they have been entrusted.

In this way, John 19:25-27 is seen to be a proclamation of how, in its maturity, the church of the martyrs and pilgrims understood the meaning of the Mother of the Lord for its present life and future hope, and especially the importance of staying at the foot of the Messiah's cross, so as to be generated ever anew by the "blood" and "water" that flow from the side of the Crucified One. So it is that we ask Mary to help us stand beneath the cross as she did, and we readily understand how the rich symbolic message of this short passage could have inspired pages of intense and loving contemplative prayer.

One example of this is the way Mary is described at the foot of the cross of her Son by Jacopone da Todi (1230/36-1306) in his *Laude* entitled *Donna de Paradiso*, a truly faith-filled rereading of John's words:

> . . . Mother, weep no more; stay and help
> Those dear to Me, the friends I leave behind.
>
> > Son, do not ask this of me; let me die with You.
> > Let me breathe my last here at Your side.
> > A common grave for son and mother,
> > Since ours is a common agony.
>
> Mother, My heart in tears, I commend you into the hands
> Of John, My chosen one; call him your son.
> John, here is My mother, take her with love;
> Have pity on her, they have pierced her heart.
>
> > My Son, You have breathed Your last;
> > Son of a mother frightened and dazed,
> > Son of a mother destroyed by grief,
> > Tortured, tormented Son!
> > Son without peer, fair and rosy-cheeked,
> > To whom shall I turn now that You have left me?
> > Why did the world so despise You?
> > Gentle and sweet Son, Son of a sorrowful mother,
> > How cruelly You have been treated!
> > John, my new son, your brother is dead:
> > The sword they prophesied has pierced my heart.
> > They have killed both mother and son,
> > One cruel death for both,
> > Embracing each other and their common cross![1]

---

1. Jacopone da Todi, *The Lauds,* trans. Serge and Elizabeth Hughes (New York: Paulist Press, 1982), p. 280.

Third Day

IN EASTER LIGHT

We now reach the third day of our retreat, the day of Jesus' resurrection and of the full revelation of the love of God the Trinity, a revelation achieved on this day by the outpouring of the Holy Spirit. We start to walk along the *via unitiva*, the experience of sharing in the divine life given from on high, which comes to full fruition in conversion of heart and in the humble yet determined desire for the holiness the Father plans for each one of us. (The aim of this day is to confirm God's work in us by the seal of the Spirit — *conformata confirmare*.) We pray using the words of the "Contemplation to Gain Love," the highpoint of Ignatius's *Spiritual Exercises:*

> Take, Lord, and receive
> All my liberty,
> My memory, my intellect,
> And all my will —
> All that I have and possess.
> Thou gavest it to me:
> And to Thee, Lord, I return it!
> All is Thine,
> Dispose of it according to all Thy will.
> Give me Thy love and Thy grace,
> For this is enough for me.[1]

1. St. Ignatius of Loyola, *Spiritual Exercises* 234.

9

The Life-Changing Encounter

In the beginning there was the experience of an encounter: Jesus showed himself alive to those who had fled on Good Friday (cf. Acts 1:3). This encounter was so decisive for them that their existence was totally transformed; fear was replaced by courage, flight by mission. Those who had fled became witnesses, remaining so until death, in a life given unconditionally to the One they had betrayed in the "hour of darkness."

Thus there is a hiatus between sunset on Good Friday and the dawn of Easter, an interruption in which something happened that was so important that it gave birth to the Christian movement in history. What had happened? While the "lay" historian can only note this "new beginning," unable to explain its causes after the failure of the various "liberal" interpretations of the Easter faith, which tended to suggest that this was a purely subjective experience of the disciples, Christian proclamation as recorded in the New Testament confesses the encounter with the Risen One to be an experience of grace — and we are offered access to this experience especially through the accounts of the appearances.

There are five groups of accounts describing the encounter with the Risen One (the Pauline tradition: 1 Cor. 15:5-8; the Marcan tradition: Mark 16:9-20; the Matthean tradition: Matt. 28:9-10, 16-20; the Lucan tradition: Luke 24:13-53; and the Johannine tradition: John 20:14-29; 21). These accounts cannot be harmonized among themselves in terms of time and place. They are, however, all constructed on the same pattern, allowing us to grasp the fundamental features of the experience to which they testify. There are always the initiative of the Risen One, the process of recognition on the part of the disciples, and then mission, which makes them witnesses of what they "heard and saw with their own eyes and contemplated and touched with their own hands" (cf. 1 John 1:1).

The *initiative* is taken by the Risen One: it is he who shows himself alive (cf. Acts 1:3), who "appears." The verbal form *ōphthē* (used in 1 Cor. 15:3-8 and Luke 24:34) may have both an active sense ("he let himself be seen, he appeared") and a passive meaning ("he was seen"). In the Greek translation of the Old Testament, however, this form of the verb is always and only used to describe theophanies, thus in the active sense of "appeared" (cf. Gen. 12:7; 17:1; 18:1; 26:2). This therefore means that what the first Christians experienced was not merely a product of their own hearts; rather, it had an "objective" character. It was something that "came" toward them, not simply something that "came to be" within them. It was not sentiments of faith and love that created their object, but the living Lord who stirred up that faith and love in a new way, transforming the very hearts of the disciples. There can thus be no philological or exegetical foundation for a reading of the resurrection like that offered, for example, by Ernest Renan, for whom "the passion of one possessed [Mary Magdalene] gave to the world a resuscitated God!"[2]

Naturally, this does not mean that there was no process of spiritual growth. Such growth was, in fact, necessary so that the first believers might "believe their own eyes" — that is, open themselves from within, in the freedom of their consciences, to what had happened in Jesus the Lord. This is the process indicated by the gradual journey of *recognition* of the Risen One *by the disciples* — carefully underlined by the New Testament texts to combat possible temptations of "enthusiasm." This is the process that led the disciples from amazement and doubt to full recognition of the Risen One: "Then their eyes were opened, and they recognized him" (Luke 24:31). This process points to the subjective and spiritual dimension of the foundational experience of the Christian faith, and it grounds the freedom of faith's assent in the encounter with the Lord Jesus. We do not believe by

2. Ernest Renan, *The Life of Jesus* (New York: Modern Library, 1955), p. 375.

ignoring our doubts, but by overcoming them in an act of trust, which, though not merely rational, also never excludes a rational reading of the signs that are offered to our awareness.

The Easter experience — inseparably both objective and subjective — is thus finally presented as an experience of *transformation*. It is the origin of the mission that will extend to the very ends of the earth. The encounter with the Risen One transforms the disciples from being those who once fled in great fear into courageous witnesses to the One who sends them: "Go into all the world and proclaim the good news to the whole creation" (Mark 16:15). Of him they speak with contagious power: "You killed the author of life, whom God raised from the dead. To this we are witnesses" (Acts 3:15). As in the case of the apostle Paul and all those who bore witness to the Risen One, it is possible to proclaim him only after we have met him, when this encounter has become for us, both in the past and in the present, a living and transforming experience.

This is an experience — both then and now — of a threefold contrast in identity: first, between the risen Christ and the One humiliated on the cross; second, between those who fled on Good Friday and who now bear witness to the Easter event; and third, between these witnesses of the Risen One and those to whom they proclaim the Word of Life so that they also may be both themselves and not themselves, thanks to this encounter that changes their lives. In the Risen One it is the Crucified who is recognized; and this recognition, which binds supreme exaltation to deepest shame, has the effect of transforming the fear of the disciples into courage. They become new persons, able to love the dignity of the new life they have received more than life itself, to the point of martyrdom. Their proclamation of this good news — which issues from a heart overflowing with joy — reaches and transforms the lives of those who believe their word, and who, thus believing, open themselves to the new life offered in Jesus, the Lord and Christ.

This is why the foundational proclamation, the *kerygma* of the good news, can be summed up in the short but deeply significant formula "Jesus the Christ," "Jesus the Lord." These words are not the mere attribution of a title to a person, but the telling of a story, the story of the way God communicated himself to humankind, and so the story of our salvation, achieved through the humiliation and exaltation of the Son of God who has come among us. By ascribing the quality of "Christ-Messiah" to the One humiliated on the cross, and by recognizing in him the *Kyrios-Adonai* whom biblical faith invoked as the God of the covenant, the Easter formula tells the story of his glorious exaltation, the Passover by which he, the One abandoned on Good Friday, is now recognized as being of the same condition as God, Lord with God's own lordship, the Savior of humankind. Thus the Easter confession of faith points to a threefold exodus of Jesus, Son of Man and Son of God: his exodus from the Father *(exitus a Deo)*; from self *(exitus a se usque ad mortem, mortem autem Crucis)*; and toward the Father *(reditus ad Deum)*.

In the first place, the Lord Jesus, who presents himself alive to his disciples, is the Son who has accepted *going out from the Father* for love of us. He is the Word who comes from Silence, the living and holy Door, who leads us into the "highest silences" of God. To receive him in faith means to listen to him in obedience, the Word made flesh, the Silence of the origins from which he comes forth. The very word "revelation" helps us grasp this, with its twofold meaning of the uncovering and at the same time the veiling of what is revealed. We are encouraged to listen to the Word who speaks in silence, and who veils while unveiling (*re-velare* means "to remove the veil" as well as "to veil anew," similarly to the Greek *apokalypsis*). Whenever this twofold reality of revelation is overlooked, it will tend to be understood as total openness (as in the German *Offenbarung*, from *offen*, to open, and from the medieval *bären*, to carry in the womb: *offenbaren* thus means "to give birth in the open," "to manifest"): the doors will thus be flung open to the ideological approach, which claims to understand everything — even the mystery of God! — and which inspired that totalitarian vision of the world, which in its turn generates all kinds of reciprocal violence.

The God of Jesus Christ, however, is not thus revealed. Indeed, he is anything but a God of total and tactless manifestation, but rather a God who rejects the proud and who can in no wise be captured in conceptual formulas intended to explain everything. The right response to the God of Jesus Christ is the attitude that the New Testament calls the "obedience of faith" (*hypakoē tēs pisteōs*), listening to what is not spoken (as the etymology suggests: *ob-audire, hypo-akouein* means to "listen to what is further, beneath, beyond"). To obey the Word in this way means listening to that Silence from which the Word issues and onto which he opens: "The Father pronounced a Word — this was his Son —, and he continually says this Word in eternal silence; thus it is that the soul must listen to the Word in silence."[3] We receive Christ, who came forth from the Father, by letting ourselves be born again from on high, in the silence of contemplative listening and in humble and faithful invocation of the living God.

In the Risen Jesus we are also given a glimpse of what it meant for him *to go out from himself,* in a journey that he traveled in perfect fidelity to abandonment on the cross — the journey of his freedom. In his acceptance of living for the Father and for humankind, Jesus was free from himself in an unconditional way; he lived this journey from himself without return out of love for the Father and humankind. It was precisely thus that he tore down the wall of enmity (cf. Eph. 2:14). At the hour of the cross, at the highpoint of his journey of freedom, Jesus offered himself as the Abandoned One, free from self out of love for the Father and for us, to the extent of accepting absolute dereliction.

Finally, Jesus *went out from this world to the Father,* in his *reditus,* or return, to the glory from which he had first come. By his resurrection he offers himself to us as the witness to the God who is Other with respect to this world, and who is the Ultimate with respect to all that is penultimate. He is the giver of the Holy Spirit, the source of that living water which makes the gift of God present here and now and which leads us human beings to the glory of him who is all in all. This third exodus of the Son of Man reminds us that Christianity is by no means the religion of the triumph of the negative, but that it is and remains, despite all and against all, the religion of hope. Thus Christians, even in a world that has lost its taste for the search for meaning, are those who have the Eternal at heart and so continue to propose the passion for saving Truth as the meaning of life and of the history of each and every human person.

The revelation offered in the resurrection of the Lord Jesus thus challenges his disciples to give an account of the hope that is in them with gen-

---

3. St. John of the Cross, *Sentenze, Spunti d'amore* 21.

tleness and respect for all (cf. 1 Pet. 3:15), letting themselves become the place where the Other breaks into the world, he who offered himself to us in the threefold exodus of the Son of Man. To his exodus must correspond our own: at the personal and community levels this means that we are to be his disciples, servants out of love and witnesses to meaning.

In the first place, the disciples of the Risen One are called to be *disciples of the Only One*. As Jesus comes forth from the Father and lives completely in obedient attention to him, so his disciples are called to affirm the primacy of God, and thus the primacy of the contemplative dimension of life, keeping their hearts ever attentive to those springs of eternity which have been revealed and offered in Christ. In the second place, the disciples of the Risen One are called to follow Jesus in his exodus from self without return, making themselves servants out of love on the model he offers when he leaves self behind and hands himself over to the Father in the supreme abandonment of the cross. His disciples are called to live in solidarity especially with the weakest and poorest of their traveling companions, never seeking somehow to escape from that history of suffering and tears in which their Lord and Master came to dwell, and where he planted his cross, so as to make present there the power of his Easter victory. Finally, as disciples of the One who returns to God the Father in his victory over death, Christians are called to be witnesses to the greater meaning of life and history, hoping in him who has opened to human beings the doors of the Kingdom. This means that they have to be ready to pay the price of bearing witness to what is ultimate in the daily struggles that bind them to the penultimate; the passion for transcendent and sovereign truth, fully revealed in the Risen One, gives birth to the church's missionary outreach.

The challenge of the living Christ thus reaches into the very depths of our hearts. Is he the Lord for me, the one who gives me life, so that I can say with Paul, "it is no longer I who live, but it is Christ who lives in me" (Gal. 2:20)? Do I draw my life from the continual and ever new encounter with him, in his Word, in the sacraments of the church, in the bonds of charity? Do I bear witness to the Risen One? Do I accord God absolute primacy in my life, desiring in all things to be the disciple of the Only One? Do I leave self behind, seeking always to make new choices of charity and service? Am I a witness to the greater meaning of life and of history, ready to give an account of that hope in the Risen One that transforms hearts and lives?

As we seek to answer these questions, we are impelled to implore the gift that flows from the Risen One for every creature — his Spirit. And so we pray, saying:

Christ,
radiant image of the Father,
prince of peace,
you who reconcile God with humankind
and humankind with God,
eternal Word made flesh,
in you alone
will we embrace God.
You who made yourself little
to let yourself slake the thirst
of our awareness and love,
give us the grace of seeking you
in all our yearnings,
of believing in you in the darkness of faith,
of looking forward to your coming in ardent hope,
and of loving you
with free and joyful hearts.
Give us the grace not to let ourselves be overcome
by the power of darkness,
or seduced by the glitter
of what passes.
And so give us your Spirit,
that he himself may become in us
longing and faith,
hope and humble love.
And so we will seek you, Lord, in the night,
we will keep vigil for you at all times,
and the days of our mortal life
will become like a bright dawn,

when you will come,
shining star of the morning,
finally to be for us
the Sun that never sets.
Amen. Alleluia!

10

The Resurrection as the
Story of the Trinity

Why does meeting the Risen One transform the disciples' lives so deeply, and why is this encounter with him capable of thus transforming the lives of those who come to believe in him? These questions can find an answer only when we begin to perceive how the Easter events involve all three Persons of the Blessed Trinity: at Easter, the Risen Jesus — filled with the Holy Spirit by the work of God the Father — pours the Spirit out on all flesh. Understood thus, the resurrection is the act by which "the God of Abraham, the God of Isaac, and the God of Jacob, the God of our ancestors" (Acts 3:13) has loved the Crucified Jesus "with power according to the Spirit of holiness" (Rom. 1:4). By this very same act, the Father demonstrates his love for us (cf. Rom. 5:8), gracing us in the Risen Christ "with every spiritual blessing," pouring out on us the gift of the Holy Spirit (cf. the hymn in Eph. 1:3-14). Thanks to this powerful love of the Father at work in the resurrection of his Son, what happened on the cross is turned upside down: where infidelity to love had triumphed in the dramatic hours of betrayal, now there triumphs the fidelity of God, who pours the Spirit of his love into our hearts (cf. Rom. 5:5); where the powers of this world and of the law had condemned One considered a subversive and blasphemer, now there reigns the freedom of the children of God and the gift of grace, which wins the day over every enslavement of life and heart (cf. Paul's "Gospel" in the letters to the Galatians and Romans).

On the cross, Jesus the Son handed the Spirit over to the Father so as to journey into the exile of sinners; now, at Easter, the Father gives the Spirit to the Son, drawing the whole world with him and in him into communion with God the Trinity. This way of understanding Easter finds expression in the well-known images of the angelic Trinity in the Christian East. The interaction of the three figures gathered around the chalice at the banquet — as, for example, in Andrej Rublev's famous icon of the Trinity — is charged with a dynamic power that is, as it were, transmitted to, and brought to fulfillment in, those who look upon the icon in faith. They in their turn become icons of the Trinity, mirroring the life of the Three here and now, thanks to the Spirit poured out at Easter and made present in that banquet of life which is the subject of the icon. The early church bore witness to this way of understanding things when it told the story of Easter in terms of the history of the Three: the Father has raised his Son in the power of the Spirit (cf. Acts 2:24; this way of putting things returns continually in Acts). Thus it is that the main characters in this new beginning of the world are the Father, the Son, and the Holy Spirit, the giver of life.

The resurrection is, in the first place, the Father's initiative. It is he who constitutes Jesus his Son "with power according to the Spirit of holiness by resurrection from the dead" (Rom. 1:4). It is the Father who loves us to the point of handing his beloved Son over to death, letting him journey into the exile experienced by sinners: "God so loved the world that he gave his only Son, so that everyone who believes in him may not perish but may have eternal life" (John 3:16). "He . . . did not withhold his own Son, but gave him up for all of us" (Rom. 8:32). This is the folly of divine love (cf. 1 Cor. 1:18-25)! God is the Father who loves the Son, and us in him, to the very point of allowing his Son to experience abandonment on the cross for our sake.

He is the God who is love (cf. 1 John 4:8-10, 16). This statement projects our faith "into the very depths of the Godhead." Beginning from the fact that in the story of our salvation it is always the Father who takes the initiative in loving, we can perceive how love is the Father's proper characteristic. He is the fountainhead and source of love, the beginning and origin of the divine life of love. Augustine calls the Father *totius Trinitatis principium*, and the fathers of the East call him *pēgē tēs agapēs*, "the source of charity." The rich language of faith here underlines the absolute freedom and complete generosity of the Father's love: only he can call forth the event of love, because he alone can begin to love without a reason — indeed he has always loved. God has always loved and will always love. Without any necessity or cause or extrinsic reason, he began loving in eternity; and without any necessity or cause or extrinsic reason, he loves now and will always go on loving. The Father is the eternal source of love, the One who loves in absolute freedom, always and forever free in love, free to love, the eternal Lover in the purest freedom of infinite love.

If the Father is where love comes from, the Son is where love is embraced. The Son, who brings obedience to perfection on the cross and in the resurrection receives the Spirit of life, is pure acceptance, eternal loving obedience, infinite gratitude. He is the one "loved . . . before the foundation of the world" (John 17:24), in whom the divine life flows in time and eternity, springing from the fullness of the Father: "Just as the Father has life in himself, so he has granted the Son also to have life in himself" (John 5:26). The eternal Lover is distinct from the eternally Beloved, who proceeds from the Lover through the overflowing fullness of his love; the Son is the Other in love, the One in whom there comes to rest the movement of infinite generosity originating in the source of love.

The Lover is the beginning of the Beloved: from Love-the-source there springs Love-that-receives, in the unbounded unity of eternal love. This process, by which the One who lives in love gives origin in indissoluble unity to the One who receives and welcomes love, is called "generation," the eternal birth of the Son, his coming from the bosom of the Father. In relation to him who is beginning and source, eternally loving Love, the Son is the one generated, the eternally Beloved; he is the Word of the Father. In God, the receptivity of love has eternal value. To accept love is no less personalizing than giving love; letting yourself be loved is love, no less than loving. The Son reveals to us that receiving, too, is divine, and that gratitude is just as divine as generosity!

Finally, in this story of everlasting love, the Spirit also has his place, when at Easter he unites the One who is generated to the One who generates, showing how the indelible distinction of love does not mean separation. He is the communion of Lover and Beloved, who also ensures the communion of the Father with his creatures, not apart from the Beloved, but precisely in and through him. The Spirit ensures that unity is stronger than distinction, and eternal joy stronger than the suffering caused by the non-love of creatures. Poured out on the Crucified One on Easter Day, the Spirit reconciles the Father with the Son abandoned on Good Friday and, in him, with the passion of the world.

We can discern here the twofold role of the Spirit in the relationship between Father and Son. If in their distinction he is the personal bond of communion, himself distinct both from the one and the other because given by the one and received by the other, in their communion he is the *condilectus* (Richard of St. Victor), beloved of the one and the other, the "third" in "love," the "ecstasy" of God, as the fathers of the East would say. In the Spirit, God goes out from himself, both at the beginning of creation ("The Spirit of God swept over the face of the waters . . .": Gen. 1:2), and at the beginning of redemption ("The Holy Spirit will come upon you . . .": Luke 1:35; cf. Matt. 1:20; "And just as he was coming up out of the water, he saw the heavens torn apart and the Spirit descending like a dove on him": Mark 1:10 and parallels), and in redemption's fulfillment (the Crucified Jesus is raised by God "with power according to the Spirit of holiness": Rom. 1:4). In this sense the Spirit brings the truth of divine love to completion, showing how love — if it is really that — is never closed or possessive, but open, a gift, an exodus from the circle of the two. We could say that in God the Spirit achieves the condition of true love, its freedom from possessiveness and jealousy: "Love is not standing there gazing into one another's eyes, but looking together towards the same goal" (Antoine de Saint-Exupéry).

So what happens at Easter reveals the history of God as Trinity as an eternal event of love, as a most pure act of everlasting and boundless love. This is not only the story of the Father, Son, and Spirit, as they reveal the life-giving way they relate to each other and the marvelous generosity of their love for the world. It is also the story of the unlimited unity of the Three who together make history. Here we contemplate the unity of the love that loves (the Father), of the love that is loved (the Son), and of the love that unites them in freedom and peace (the Spirit; cf. 1 John 4:7-16). When we take as our starting point this revelation of Loving, Loved, and

Unifying Love, which is the story of Easter, then we can affirm that the only God is Love, in the indelible Trinitarian distinction between the Lover, the Beloved, and Personal Love.

This is how Augustine understood it: "In truth, when you see love, you are seeing the Trinity."[4] "Behold, they are three: the Lover, the Beloved and Love."[5] "And they are not more than three: there is the one who loves the one who comes from him, and there is the one who loves the one he comes from, and there is love itself. And if this were nothing, then how could God be love? And if this were to be without substance, then how could God be substance?"[6] Thus it is that the unique essence of the living God is his love in the eternal movement of going out from self as the Love that loves, of accepting self as the Love that is loved, and of return to self and infinite openness to the other in freedom as the Spirit of Trinitarian love. The essence of the Christian God is this everlasting dynamism of love. The Trinity is this eternal story of love and of beauty without end, which calls forth and takes upon itself and pervades the history of the world: "In the Trinity," Augustine again affirms, "is found the supreme source of all things, perfect beauty, complete joy."[7]

When Jesus' disciples find themselves standing before this abyss of God the Trinity who is Love, who by loving them calls them in their turn to love, their response can only be to celebrate the glory of so great a love. In the biblical tradition, this is what, at its deepest, is meant by confessing God's unity and uniqueness. This confession — which unites Christians to Jews and Muslims — is much more than professing an abstract idea. It is an act of adoration and at the same time a life commitment. "Hear, O Israel: The Lord is our God, the Lord alone. You shall love the Lord your God with all your heart, and with all your soul, and with all your might" (Deut. 6:4-5). For us to believe in God means to enter into the mystery of his unity

---

4. Augustine, *De Trinitate* 8.8.12: "*Immo vero vides Trinitatem, si caritatem vides.*"

5. Augustine, *De Trinitate* 8.10.14: "*Et illic igitur tria sunt: amans, et quod amatur, et amor.*"

6. Augustine, *De Trinitate* 6.5.7: "*Et ideo non amplius quam tria sunt: unus diligens eum qui de illo est, et unus diligens eum de quo est, et ipsa dilectio. Quae si nihil est, quomodo Deus dilectio est? Si non est substantia, quomodo Deus substantia est?*"

7. Augustine, *De Trinitate* 6.10.12: "*In illa enim Trinitate summa origo est rerum omnium et perfectissima pulchritudo et beatissima delectatio.*"

and to commit ourselves to working so that all women and men may enjoy justice and peace. But we can do this only when God in his very unity opens his heart to us as the unity of loving Love, of beloved Love, and of personal Love, which unites God and the world in freedom.

At this point monotheism demands, as it were, the Trinity, the confession that the God who is one is Love and takes to himself what is different from himself into the unceasing dynamism of Love without end. Confessing that God is one means entering into God's unity ourselves, but to do this means letting ourselves be taken up into God's eternal story of Love. This is what happens in prayer: Christians do not pray to a distant, foreign God; instead, they prayer *in* God, to the Father in the Spirit through the Son, receiving everything from the Father through Christ in the same Spirit. Prayer places the person at prayer in the very depths of the Trinity, and so in that unity of eternal Love which makes us able to love. Whoever prays *in* God can thus sense how taking Judaism's monotheism to its ultimate consequences leads in the end to the Christian confession of the Trinity.

Contemplating the holy mystery thus becomes a challenge to our freedom and a question for our faith and love: What place do I really recognize in my life for the spiritual experience of the Holy Trinity, revealed at Easter, to let myself be molded by the one love of the Three, which frees me from possessiveness and from being closed in on myself and makes me capable of starting ever anew in giving myself?

From Elisabeth of the Trinity, a woman in love with the Thrice-Holy God, we borrow these words to adore the God who is love and to ask for the gift of living only by this love:

> My God, Trinity I adore,
> help me to be so entirely forgetful of self
> as to be established in you,
> in quiet peace —
> as if my soul were already in eternity;
> let nothing disturb this peace
> or lead me away from you,
> my unchanging Good,

and lead me deeper at every moment
into the depths of your mystery.
Give my soul peace, make it your heaven,
your favorite dwelling-place
where you delight to rest:
Let me never leave you;
but let me be entirely in you,
ever vigilant in faith,
in complete adoration,
in complete abandonment to your creative work. . . .
O my Three, my All, my Beatitude,
Infinite Solitude, Immensity in which I lose myself,
I consign myself to you as a prey.
Bury me in you that I may bury myself in you,
while I await the time
when in your light I shall come to contemplate
the abyss of your greatness. Amen![8]

8. *Elevation to the Blessed Trinity,* November 21, 1904.

11

Moses and the Passover of Freedom:
Lectio Divina on Exodus 3:1-15 and 14:5–15:20

On this day of our retreat, our contemplation of the Trinity — manifested in all its fullness in Jesus' death and resurrection — leads us to meditate on the Christian life as an Easter existence. It is appropriate that today, out of all that "cloud of witnesses" (Heb. 12:1) who are our companions on the road, we should look especially to Moses, "saved from the waters," who led his people in their journey of liberation from the slavery of Egypt toward the land promised by God, passing through the waters of the Red Sea, which opened wonderfully to let him pass.

The Bible tells us that Moses enjoyed a uniquely privileged relationship with the Eternal One. While others were allowed only to glimpse God from behind, Moses was God's friend and spoke with the Eternal One "face to face" (Exod. 33:11; Deut. 34:10; Num. 12:8). In an expression of God's tender care for this man, a midrashic tradition tells of "Moses' little door," located beneath the throne of the Most High; when the angels — generally so well-behaved — are suddenly possessed by envy of God's special love for Moses and are looking for a way to make life difficult for him, the Lord pushes the little door open with his foot and ushers the disconcerted Moses inside, so that no harm may befall him (*Exodus rabbah* 42.5).

The unique place occupied by Moses in the heart of the Eternal One is reflected in the way he is venerated in the whole Jewish tradition. The book of Deuteronomy assures us that the long-awaited Messiah will be like a new Moses (18:15: "The Lord your God will raise up for you a prophet like me from among your own people; you shall heed such a prophet"). In the New Testament, too, Moses occupies a place of some importance, so much so that he is mentioned a full eighty times! Paul, in particular, says (in 1 Cor. 10:1ff.) that our fathers were all under the cloud, crossed the sea, and were baptized in Moses *(eis ton Mōusēn)*, clearly finding in him a symbol of the Christ who will come, in whom we in our turn are to be baptized.

Gregory of Nyssa draws on this wealth of imagery in his very beautiful *Life of Moses*, in which the patriarch is portrayed as a model of virtuous perfection and an excellent example for all of us in the journey we have to undertake in order to be pleasing to God, living as baptized persons — saved, like Moses, from the waters! — in a Passover pilgrimage, a kind of continual exodus from the slavery of our Egypt to the freedom of the land promised by God. According to Gregory, Moses on the holy mountain experienced the "bright darkness" of a mystical experience of the divine (2.163), because he was "on fire with love of beauty" (2.231) and never ceased to walk forward toward the vision of God: "To see God means to experience a desire for Him which is never satisfied . . . our thirst for what is good increases despite being slaked" (2.239). Precisely because he always went on growing in this way, Moses was a "model of beauty," teaching us to bear witness like him to "the seal of the beauty which has been shown us" (2.319).

Following Jewish tradition, chapter 7 of the Acts of the Apostles (verses 20-43) divides the life of Moses into three periods, each of forty years: verse 23 says that "when he was forty years old, it came into his heart to visit his relatives, the Israelites"; verse 30 states that "now when forty years had passed, an angel appeared to him in the wilderness of Sinai, in the flame of a burning bush." In the book of Deuteronomy it is the dying Moses himself who says: "I am now one hundred and twenty years old" (31:2; cf. 34:7). So, according to this very rich biblical tradition, Moses' long life is made up of forty years at Pharaoh's court, forty years in the land of Midian, and forty years in the desert. The number forty — arrived at by multiplying four, the number of the world's cardinal points, by ten, the number of divine perfection — is full of symbolic meaning: each of the three periods of forty years, it is suggested, has its own universally applicable meaning. In each of these periods all human beings will be able to recognize something of themselves and to reread their own lives as they actually are and as they should be before God. In this way, biblical tradition expresses the conviction that Moses stands for all of us, called to live with the life of the Trinity, to the praise of the God who is Love!

The first period of forty years could be called *the time of utopia:* in other words, these are the years of sweet ingenuousness, when Moses, saved from the waters by Pharaoh's daughter and brought up as a refined young man (cf. Exod. 2 and Acts 7), lives in a coddled, protected world. This is the time for dreams and great expectations, when Moses' perception of life and of the people around him is, as it were, filtered and is hence at least partially an illusion. Moses starts to dream about changing the world. He knows — because his Hebrew nurse, who is in fact his mother, must certainly have told him — that he is an Israelite; and, as the bright, rich, and happy young man that he is, he conceives in his heart the dream of being the one who will liberate his people. In the "sweet unawareness" of this time in his life, there can be no doubt that he is seeking more his own glory than the true freedom of his people, whom in fact he does not yet really know at all. This is the Moses who leaves Pharaoh's court to go into the midst of the children of Israel, to whom he knows he belongs.

However, as soon as he steps outside of Pharaoh's palace, something unexpected happens. Our hero comes across an insufferable scene, with an Egyptian beating a Hebrew, one of his brothers. Moses is indignant. Right in front of him, the liberator who has come to see justice done, this Egyptian takes it upon himself to strike a son of Israel! Moses is possessed by the temptation (until then unknown to him) of using violence, and — not even really knowing what he is doing — he kills the Egyptian, only to regret at once what he has done and hide the body almost as if to cancel the deed he has done.

The following day a Hebrew strikes a brother Hebrew in Moses' presence. Moses would like to intervene to remind them of the brotherhood that unites them. He is, however, met with an unexpected and cutting response: "Do you want to kill me now as you killed the Egyptian?" Moses' own brothers now begin to reject him; he has become acutely inconvenient for them. Moses, who ingenuously thought he could change the world and who has fallen immediately into the typical trap of taking ideological shortcuts, begins to understand how hard and difficult reality truly is. Moses experiences the great pain of defeat: the naive dreamer, the young man who has experienced sweet unawareness, comes to know all the heaviness of reality. Here begins *his time of disenchantment*. This is the second stage of Moses' life, the season of defeat. Great expectations soon give way to disillusionment. As the Acts of the Apostles so baldly notes: "He supposed that his kinsmen would understand that through him God was rescuing them, but they did not understand" (Acts 7:25). In that "but" is contained all the bitterness of his frustration, the crisis of the life he had dreamed of (cf. vv. 27-29).

Moses experiences the intense pain of becoming a "stranger" to everyone: to Pharaoh, because he is now a rebel; to his own people, because his courage makes them afraid, inasmuch as they fear that he will place in jeopardy the precarious equilibrium of their slavery; to himself, because he understands that he has to flee, without knowing where. The hero who had given up a privileged life knows fear and takes flight: "When he heard this, Moses fled and became a resident alien in the land of Midian" (Acts 7:29). In the land of his exile he gradually settles down; he thinks he has done enough, gives up the dreams of his youth, and considers that he has won the right to a quiet life, without further surprises or risks. This is the time when failure leads to resignation, and his outward exile runs the risk of working its way into his heart. And yet, the forty years in Midian are also a time for drawing up a balance sheet, for growth in maturity, for solitude with God in the desert, as Gregory of Nyssa underlines. In disillusionment, Moses is prepared for the mission of his maturity.

Now comes his third stage, *his time of faith and of greater love*, which begins with a radical turning point, marked by God's eruption into his life: "Now when forty years had passed, an angel appeared to him in the wilderness of Mount Sinai, in the flame of a burning bush" (Acts 7:30). Apparently unexpectedly — but actually the fruit of a slow, deep growth in maturity, indicative of a soul that has not ceased to be noble and open to mystery — Moses discovers God's initiative and understands that, even if he himself does not want to take an interest in God, God is still interested in him. At this point the great events happen that will make Moses the forerunner of the Messiah and of every person baptized in Christ.

The first of these events is his experience of the "burning bush" (Acts 7:30-31; Exod. 3:1-15; cf. Exod. 6:2-13 and 6:28–7:7). We need here above all to underline Moses' *amazement*. He is tending his flock near Mount Sinai and suddenly sees a bush that burns without being consumed. "He approached to look . . .": this is important, because it tell us that Moses, even though he has been through so much, is still capable of surprise. At eighty years of age he is still capable of experiencing wonder, of being open to what is new! In this sense he is a radically human person, in search of the Mystery: where there is awe, there is this openness to the new things God does, to his impossible possibility! Only where awe does not exist is there no more life, no more surprise. Moses has never given up being a pilgrim, a searcher; even though he has settled down in exile, his heart still goes on secretly yearning for home and for the beauty he has yet to encounter.

It is at this point that *God's call* comes: "Moses! Moses!" God calls us by name. None of us is anonymous for God. Each of us is a "you" — absolutely unique, singular, loved infinitely. Moses experiences himself as loved personally by God. This is no experience of wanting to take hold of God for oneself: on the contrary, the admonition is clear, "Come no closer! Remove the sandals from your feet" (Exod. 3:4-6). It is instead a matter of letting yourself be taken hold of by God, because only God can make the desert into holy land! "I will send you." It is no longer Moses who is the prime mover, who makes the decisions and claims to be able to change the world; it is God who sends him. "Go to Pharaoh." As if nothing had gone before, as if he had never experienced failure, Moses accepts this new beginning. God makes possible the impossible: his name is a promise, "I am who I am," "I will be with you," the faithful God (v. 14). Moses had not asked for a definition of God's essence; he had asked God to commit himself for him and his people. The holy and blessed Name is thus a guarantee, founded in the reality of God's fidelity, and on such a foundation Moses can begin his adventure.

It is at this point that Moses experiences the *test of his faith*, the crossing of the Red Sea (Exod. 14:5–15:20; cf. 1 Cor. 10:1-2; Heb. 11:29). Before him is the sea with its high waves; behind him is Pharaoh with his chariots and horsemen. In such circumstances, human logic would counsel calculation, the choice of compromise. Moses is afraid. Humanly speaking, the alternative is between death in the sea and submission to Pharaoh (cf. Exod. 14:10-14). The choice is imposed: either to trust God or to calculate by human logic. Moses has no hesitation in involving the people and encouraging them: "Do not be afraid, stand firm, and see the deliverance the Lord will accomplish for you today" (v. 13). Yet he remains alone before God, bearing an enormous burden, because to trust God now may look like failing to take proper action. In his loneliness he cries out to his God, so much so that the Most High asks him: "Why do you cry out to me?" (v. 15). And yet he goes on bearing witness to the people that he trusts the fidelity of the Eternal One: "The Lord will fight for you" (v. 14). Moses is now a true leader, because he realizes that what he can allow himself to be and to say in direct interaction with God he must temper with the wisdom of love when he speaks to his people; we must never unload our own crosses onto the shoulders of those who are weaker! And Moses understands that there is another possibility: to believe in God in spite of everything, in spite of God's apparent defeat.

So Moses reaches the most important moment, and the most significant act, of his life: he trusts God, he believes against all the evidence to the contrary. Making his leap of faith in the dark, he obeys the Lord, who says: "Tell the Israelites to go forward. But you lift up your staff, and stretch out your hand over the sea and divide it, that the Israelites may go into the sea on dry ground" (vv. 15-16). The waters of the sea roll back, the people pass through them unharmed, and the Egyptians who are pursuing them are overwhelmed. The symbolism employed here is tragic and very hard: the waters of life for the Hebrews are the waters of death for the Egyptians. Moses, leader in the faith that passes through the sea, is saved from the waters together with his people. It is then that he experiences faith's victory: in the night, trusting blindly, seeing nothing, he witnesses the royal Passover, and from his heart there erupts his song of gratitude, the song of the saved (cf. Exod. 15). From then on Moses will always be what he was on that night at the Red Sea: the man of intercession and responsibility (cf. Exod. 17), the man of the Word (cf. Exod. 19:3), who suffers out of love for his people and out of love for his God, in a continual, hope-filled exodus toward the land of God's promise.

Moses' life draws to a close when he is 120 years old. As Deuteronomy tells it, Moses dies alone, in obedience to God, without entering the promised land: "The Lord addressed Moses as follows: 'Ascend this mountain of the Abarim, Mount Nebo, which is in the land of Moab, across from Jericho, and view the land of Canaan, which I am giving to the Israelites for a possession; you shall die there on the mountain that you ascend" (Deut. 32:48-50). One cannot but be moved by Moses' solitary death, in obedience to God: "Then Moses, the servant of the Lord, died there in the land of Moab, at the Lord's command" (Deut. 34:5). In solitude, in the cold of the mountain, Another will receive him and will be his warmth. And while he will let Moses see the Promised Land from afar, he will give him the Land of which this is only the symbol. Moses' death — like the Christian's, saved too from the waters and so guardian of hope in the Risen One — is no mere going down of the sun, but the dawn of life. It is a *dies natalis,* a birthday and not a day of ending, the threshold where the divine Other calls us into our last exodus and welcomes us into the fulfillment that is Easter without end.

So Moses challenges all of us who have been saved in the waters of baptism and redeemed by the Passover of Jesus: Where are we in our journey of faith? What stage are we at? Have we really gone past the stage of utopias, which for the humankind of which we are a part was the time of ideologies and "emancipated" modernity? Have we moved on from disillusionment or do we still experience it, as we travel with the women and men of our time? Have we entered deep into the night of faith? Have we crossed our Red Sea with Jesus, the new Moses? Have we set out with determination in his company toward God's promised land? Are we leading with fidelity and hope those who have been entrusted to our care?

Humbly and confidently we ask the Lord, who has freed his people and guides them to ever new freedom, to grant this grace to us as well, plunging us unceasingly into the ocean of his infinite love. And we do this taking our inspiration from these words of Gregory of Nyssa:

Make us like Moses, Lord, passionately in love with beauty. As we gladly receive all that is given us as an image of the One for whom we yearn, we make so bold as to ask that we may yet thirst to be filled with Beauty itself, which transcends all our desires, so as to enjoy it not in mirrors and reflections, but face to face. . . . As you did for Moses, allow us also to understand that we are truly seeing Your Face when, while seeing it, we never stop yearning to see it more. . . . Amen. Alleluia! (*Life of Moses* 2.232-33)

12

Mary, Ark of the Covenant: *Lectio Divina* on Luke 1:39-45

At the annunciation, Mary was wrapped in the loving embrace of the Trinity, she welcomed the Son of God into her womb, and so she became the mother of the Messiah. In this way, she also became the perfect image of what it means for a creature to be inhabited by grace, as well as the image of the new creation that the Word and the Spirit, sent into the world, bring about in history and in the lives of human beings. It is insights such as these that the evangelist Luke intends to share with his readers, when, immediately after the annunciation, he tells of the visit paid by Mary to Elizabeth. Full of the presence of the Most High, the Virgin Mother shares this presence in works of charity. The mysterious way in which the first sound of Mary's voice makes Elizabeth's child leap for joy in her womb tells of how Mary's heart is truly overflowing with longing to share the gift of love and new life she has received through the kindness of the God now dwelling in her. Thus to contemplate what happened at the visitation will help us understand what happens in the life of the Lord's disciples when they put their faith in the church's proclamation of the Easter faith, and so let themselves be led deep into the life of the Trinity, to become transparent and loving witnesses of that same Trinity among their fellow human beings.

Luke 1:39-45 tells the story both soberly and with intellectual rigor. This brief text represents a highly developed piece of biblical theology, crafted to confirm all the central elements of the annunciation. The way Luke writes of the visitation is clearly modeled on the account of the transfer of the ark of the covenant to Jerusalem, as this is described in the second book of Samuel (2 Sam. 6:2-16). There are striking similarities between the two texts. Both events take place in the same geographical area, the region of Judah (cf. 2 Sam. 6:1-2 and Luke 1:39). In both episodes there are manifestations of joy: David is "dancing before the Lord" (2 Sam. 6:5); he transports the ark "with rejoicing" (v. 12); he leaps and dances (vv. 14, 16); the baby in Elizabeth's womb "leaped for joy" (Luke 1:41, 44). This joy is translated into acclamations, which have a liturgical feel: "David brought up the ark of the Lord with shouting, and with the sound of the trumpet" (2 Sam. 6:15); "Elizabeth was filled with the Holy Spirit and exclaimed with a loud cry . . ." (Luke 1:41-42; it should be noted that the verb *anaphōnein* — "to shout, to cry out" in v. 42 is used by the Septuagint only for liturgical acclamations: cf. 1 Chron. 16:4, 5, 42). The presence of the ark in the house of Obed-edom the Gittite is a source of blessing (cf. 2 Sam. 6:11-12: "The Lord blessed Obed-edom and all his household"), as is the arrival of Mary in the house of Zechariah ("Elizabeth was filled with the Holy Spirit": Luke 1:41). Just as David is taken by a sense of religious fear before the ark (2 Sam. 6:9: "How can the ark of the Lord come into my care?"), so is Elizabeth in the presence of Mary ("Why has this happened to me, that the mother of my Lord has come to me?": Luke 1:43). Finally, the ark remains in the house of Obed-edom for three months (cf. 2 Sam. 6:11: "The ark of the Lord remained three months in the house of Obed-edom the Gittite"), and Mary stays "about three months" (Luke 1:56) in the house of Elizabeth. The theological insight that emerges from this parallelism is one of great intensity and beauty: Mary is the ark of the new covenant (*foederis arca,* as she is called by the church), the place of the saving presence of God-with-us, just as the account of the virginal conception had already led us to understand.

The expression placed on Elizabeth's lips by which she calls Mary "the mother of my Lord" (Luke 1:43) explicitly confirms all this: the Easter title *Kyrios* — "Lord," used nineteen times in the Gospel of Luke to refer to Jesus, speaks of his condition as Messiah-King, Savior, and God. Mary is the mother of the One whom God has made "both Lord and Christ" by raising him from the dead (cf. Acts 2:36), the "Son of God" among us (cf. Luke 1:35), the Savior, Jesus (cf. v. 31). And she is all this — Luke loves to point out — because she is a believer, the image of the true disciple, "blessed" because she "believed that there would be a fulfillment of what was spoken to her by the Lord" (v. 45). Ark of the new and definitive covenant between the Eternal One and his people, mother of the Messiah of divine condition and Savior, Mary is not only the place where God comes among us; in her shines forth his loving and transforming presence, because she is the Mother of Beautiful Love, who makes the children of God beautiful in the Son and shares with them her certainty of being loved in the Beloved, and of being loved thus so as to be able to love. The Virgin who receives the Son of God in faith is also the Mother who gives generously in love: it is precisely thus that Mary, Virgin and Mother, images for us what it means to be a disciple transformed by grace and shows us what to look for in those new creatures made possible by the Incarnation and the Passover of the Word.

What, then, are the traits of these new creatures? If we take up the great patristic and theological tradition that has provided us with numerous commentaries on the visitation, we can identify seven characteristics that emerge in Mary here and that point to what can happen in persons who put their faith in the love of God the Trinity.

The first is Mary's *attentiveness.* The young mother of the Messiah understands the needs of her cousin, who has become pregnant at an advanced age, and goes quickly to her aid. Mary does not wait to be asked for her help, nor does she need Elizabeth to put her need into words. Mary sees things with love and so knows what needs to be done. *Ubi amor, ibi oculus:* when there is love, the eye sees what it would never see without love. To be attentive means to learn to be vigilantly ready to help the other person, quick to become aware of others' needs, sensitive to their unspoken suffering, generously ready to give of oneself without waiting for appeals or laws. Attentiveness begins in the heart and can be created there only by the Holy Spirit, who has been sent to pour out on us the love of the Father (cf. Rom. 5:5). It is no accident that St. Ambrose makes this comment on the visitation: "The grace of the Spirit, whose most important fruit is love, does not tarry, nor does it know delay."[9]

---

9. St. Ambrose, *Expositio in Evangelium secundum Lucam* 2.19: *"Nescit tarda molimina Spiritus Sancti gratia, cuius praecipuus fructus amor est."*

In Mary, attentiveness goes hand in hand with the *perceptiveness that is born of love.* This is the ability to listen to, and understand, the mystery of the other person and to respond to that mystery with deeds that are true. Mary does not seek to categorize Elizabeth nor to draw up some abstract plan of action; rather, she simply goes to her and creates such a deep mutual understanding with her that her voice becomes a bridge between their two hearts, in a conversation that somehow even involves the babies they carry in their wombs. When the Bible speaks of this kind of loving perceptiveness it talks of the human "heart," dwelling place of the real treasure that is each of us, the only place where authentic and true human encounter can happen: *cor ad cor loquitur.* As Antoine de Saint-Exupéry says, "what is essential is invisible to the eyes: only the heart can see it." Mary, the Mother of Beautiful Love, has a heart able to recognize the essential in herself and in others, and she knows how to respond with supple spontaneity.

As a consequence, what she in fact does is marked with a refreshing *practicality.* She does not daydream about what good thing she might or might not do, nor does she anguish over what she might or might not become, all the while passing up the opportunity to do some practical good for her neighbor. The opposite of this down-to-earth practicality is ideology, in which I look at life and the world as if each individual person were only one more exemplification of a universal truth and thus feel justified in applying generalized norms without respect or love. Mary, instead, is practical because she obeys the truth that her loving perceptiveness has led her to know, and she acts in consequence, without alibi or escape. This attitude of hers is wonderfully expressed where Luke's account notes that the Mother of Jesus "set out and went with haste to a Judean town in the hill country" — that is, to the place where Elizabeth lived (v. 39). The expression "with haste" *(meta spoudēs)* speaks of all the concern and care with which Mary puts her heart's decision into action. The participle *anastasa,* which literally means "having arisen" and evokes the language of the resurrection, indicates how her haste was no last-minute improvisation or fussiness — doing something just for the sake of needing to do something — but flowed rather from outgoing love, from the hidden depths of a heart that has learned to help.

Fourth, Mary at the visitation acts with *joy*. She is moved to visit her cousin by a love so fresh and radiant that it fills her and her voice with a river of joy that flows into the lives of those she meets. The mother of the Messiah does not act out of any sense of having to do a duty or of being obliged to act by the turn events have taken. In her everything is a gift freely given, goodness that is shared, generosity without calculation or constraint. To know joy is to experience oneself as loved so deeply as to be able to love, to respond to the love received beyond any measure with the love given without condition or reserve. Inhabited by the love of the Three, ark of the divine presence, the Virgin Mother gives freely what she freely received; in her all is grace, and so all is joy.

Precisely thus, what Mary does here is full of *tenderness*. This speaks of the effect the Virgin Mary's love has on those whose lives it touches. Elizabeth and the child in her womb are flooded with joy. Love's tenderness does not create distance; it gathers to itself those who are far off, makes them feel at home, and fills them with the amazement and beauty of discovering that they are loved so generously without any merit of their own, as a sheer gift. "And why has this happened to me, that the mother of my Lord comes to me? For as soon as I heard the sound of your greeting, the child in my womb leaped for joy" (Luke 1:43-44). Tenderness means giving with joy so as to evoke joy in the beloved; it means "infecting" others with freedom and peace. Those who love without tenderness create dependency or remain aloof in a way that means that joy cannot come to birth.

Sixth, there is *gift* — the generosity that inspires Mary's whole behavior here. She gives everything, not simply a part of herself, but her own self. She asks for nothing in exchange; she does not expect anything back. Mary helps us to understand that God's grace is never a privilege, but a task. It is not given to us to keep it shut up in our own inner world, but so that it can shine out, so that we can pour it out on others as generously as it has been poured out on us. Life's meaning and beauty lie in this movement of generosity, of love without a reason — or, better, of love that has no other reason than the simple irradiating power of love itself.

Finally, there is *silence*. The visitation certainly opens with words of greeting, the grateful exclamation of the Baptist's mother: "Blessed are you among women, and blessed is the fruit of your womb" (Luke 1:42), and it also climaxes in Mary's song, her "Magnificat." And yet what happens during Mary's three months with Elizabeth is shrouded in silence. This silence tells of the ordinariness of the time the two women spent together, united in the marvelous complicity of expecting their sons' births. The things done in this silence, though, in some ways speak louder than words. One might even say that Mary's song of joy celebrates what she and her kinswoman experienced in that house in the Judean hill country — the wonders the Eternal God had begun to accomplish in the womb of the Messiah's mother. This silence says that being comes before doing, truth before appearance; first place goes to the love of all those who put their faith in the Easter gift of God the Trinity and let themselves be hidden with Christ in God's heart. Taught by Mary, the Mother of Beautiful Love, we learn the essential simplicity of goodness, its deep power going to the root of things and from there spreading out without fanfare or bright lights.

So the Virgin of the visitation challenges us to look at the truth of who we really are: Am I attentive to other people, to the other person? Do I try to live with loving perceptiveness, not focusing on appearances but seeing the heart? Am I practical in the decisions I make and in the way I behave in charity, as a fruit of the love poured out in me by the Spirit of the Risen One? Do I live in the joy of knowing that I am loved with and in Christ by the Father? Am I respectful and tactful in all my relationships, making no distinction of persons, not creating distance, and neither creating nor assenting to enslaving dependencies? Am I moved by generosity in my choices, or do I try to make a name for myself rather than for Christ and the poor? Do I try to please God in the silent eloquence of deeds, without seeking to create an image for myself or hiding behind masks intended somehow to protect me?

May the Virgin Mother of love help us to give a truthful response to these questions and, as she did, to accord love the first place in our lives as disciples of the Risen One, witnesses of the Trinity. To her we address this humble but ardent request for her intercession and help, borrowing the words of Francesco Petrarca:

Most glorious Virgin, you are clothed in glory
and crowned with stars; you pleased the highest Sun

so very much He hid His light in you;
you are the theme to which love drives me on.
But how, without your help, can I begin,
and His Who, loving, hid Himself in you?
(I call on her who always answers to
the prayers of faithful men.)
Our Lady, if the extreme
of human misery can always turn
your eyes to us in mercy, hear my prayer;
succour me in my war,
though I am dust, and you are heaven's queen.[10]

10. Petrarch, *Canzoniere*, trans. J. G. Nichols, no. 366, "Vergine bella, che di sol vestita," stanza 1 (New York: Routledge, 2002), p. 305.

Fourth Day

IN THE CHURCH
THAT IS COMMUNION

On this fourth day of our spiritual exercises, we intend to reach for a deeper understanding and awareness of what it means for us to be given a share in the life of the Trinity: the light of the Risen Christ makes us one with the children of the light in the church of love. This *via unitiva*, which calls for a transformation of our person, leads here and now to a new way of relating to other persons. Because the gift we receive is communion with the blessed Trinity, it finds expression in a new relationship of unity. (In the language of the spiritual tradition, this is the moment when our task is to *confirmata transformare*, to translate the new life we have received as a gift into genuine and transforming relationships with others.) This is the day of the church, and we would like to begin it, echoing the unanimous tradition of the fathers, by making our own the prayer of a holy African bishop who died in exile at Naples, where he had been received with love:

> Lord, grant that we may all
> love your church, the beloved.
> Let us remain
> unfailingly faithful to her
> as to a loving, attentive, and kind mother,
> so that with her and through her
> we may become worthy

of finding our home with you,
our God and Father.
Amen.[1]

1. St. Quodvultdeus of Carthage, *On the Profession of Faith for Those Aspiring to Baptism* 3.12-13.

13

Ecclesia de trinitate

The church that Jesus came to found on earth is the community of God's sons and daughters who have been made such in the Son, the community of those loved in the Beloved. It is the church of love. This is clearly expressed by a word used especially by the Gospel of John, the comparative conjunction *kathōs*, "as." Jesus uses this word when he is talking about the kind of relationship existing between him and his disciples, as well as the relationship between them and the communion in which he always lives with the Father: "This is my commandment, that you love one another *as* I have loved you" (John 15:12; cf. 13:34); "... that they may all be one. *As* you, Father, are in me and I am in you" (John 17:21-22).

Jesus' use of the word shows how many levels of meaning it can in fact have: *kathōs* indicates a relationship that is at once causal, exemplary, and final, and thus it speaks of how the Trinity is the source, the model, and the goal of the communion existing among Jesus' disciples, which is the church. In the light of this *kathōs*, we can say that the church comes from the love of the Trinity *(ecclesia de Trinitate),* is the image of the Trinity's shared life *(ecclesia communio sanctorum),* and journeys toward the Trinity in history *(ecclesia viatorum).*

Everything in the church comes from the thrice-holy God. The very heart of the church is *agapē,* the love that comes from above and tends to return on high. *Agapē* is the rule of life of Jesus' disciples, who have put their faith in the power of his revelation of the Father's infinite love. *Kathōs* helps us understand that the church draws the power of its deepest life from letting itself be loved by the Father through Christ in the Spirit, so as then to love the Father through Christ in the same Spirit. Loved in the Beloved, we are loved so as to be able to love. This is why in John *kathōs* is linked to another expression — the pronoun of reciprocity *allēlon/allēlous* — "one another." We show forth the love shared with us by the Three when we love one another. This love for one another is the other face of that one love which creates the church. If *kathōs* speaks of the relationship between the Trinity and ourselves, *allēlon/allēlous* speaks of the relationship of reciprocity between us. God's love creates fraternal love!

Bearing this in mind, we can take our meditation on the church forward in three directions: first, by calling to mind how the church comes to be; second, by becoming more deeply aware of what happens in the church in our own "meantime"; and third, by looking forward to the home promised us and for which we long. In other words, we can ask: Where does the church come from? What is the church? And where is the church going?

In this meditation we will contemplate the first question, *where does the church come from?* To answer this question, we have to seek a deeper awareness of how the church comes into being. In faith we contemplate God's loving initiative as it reaches us in the story of the revelation brought to fulfillment in Jesus Christ. God's love precedes human love: the church is not the fruit of "flesh and blood," nor a flower that has blossomed from this earth, but a gift from above, the fruit of God's own initiative. The church was eternally present in the Father's mind; as he planned our salvation, he prepared for the birth of the church in the history of his covenant with Israel, so that, once the times were fulfilled, the church would be the place where he would pour out the Holy Spirit.

The church — like its Lord — is *oriens ex alto*: it does not have its origin here, neither in some sort of coming together of human interests, nor in the zeal of some generous heart. Its origin is from "on high," with God, whence came the Son in the flesh to give life to this flesh in the immortal and transforming power of the Trinity's life. With the Easter event, the Spirit entered in a full and final way into the history of this world. God "found time for humankind," and, with the dawn of the resurrection, the days of our human history became penultimate time, the "meantime" between the first coming of the Son of Man and his return in glory, the time of the Spirit tirelessly at work in human history. The church was born because the Son and the Spirit were sent, and thus it is a real sharing in the life of the Trinity in human history: *"De unitate Patris et Filii et Spiritus Sancti plebs adunata"* ("A people gathered in the unity of the Father, of the Son and of the Holy Spirit"; St. Cyprian, *De Oratione Dominica* 23)!

The tradition of the Christian East offers us a particularly powerful image here when it points out that, after the self-emptying of the Word in the darkness of the flesh, there followed the self-emptying of the Spirit in the darkness of the Bridegroom. If the *kenosis* of the Son is such as to conceal and at the same time reveal his divinity in the countenance of the man Jesus, the *kenosis* of the Spirit consists in the fact that the countenances of the redeemed bear witness — even if still amid the contradictions of this mortal life — to their being "divinized" by the Paraclete. The unseen Father now speaks to humankind in the countenance of the Word incarnate and in the countenances of the disciples of the Beloved, transfigured from within by the gift of Christ's Spirit. This mysterious and eloquent *kenosis* of the third divine Person is the church, related by a far from weak analogy to the other *kenosis* of the eternal Son who has come in the flesh (cf. *Lumen Gentium,* 8). The church is the tent God has pitched among humankind, the presence of the Trinity in history, generated ever anew "from above" by the Trinity's gift of love. From the fact that the church comes from God in this way derive practical and important consequences for the church understood respectively as gift, mystery, and commitment.

In the first place, the church's origin "from on high" shows how she is above all *a gift and a grace:* the church neither invents nor produces herself; instead, she receives herself. She is the fruit not of any human effort but of the generous offer of a grace that is neither merited nor predictable. The church is born from receptivity and gratitude. The consequence of this is that she must live in a way that is both contemplative and eucharistic. Wherever God is adored in persevering expectation, wherever gratitude is celebrated in the powerful memory of his great deeds and the Crucified and Risen One becomes present here and now among his own, the Spirit breaks through and creates the family of the children of God.

When this contemplative dimension of the Christian life is given priority, this always nourishes and regenerates the church afresh. The fathers of the church express this conviction through the very beautiful image of the church as the "moon." The church is the moon because she shines in the world's night by the light of the sun alone, who is Christ; his rays bathe the church and make her shine as a light for the peoples. As St. Ambrose writes, "This is the true moon, which receives the light of immortality and grace from her brother-star which never sets. In fact the Church does not shine by her own light, but by the light of Christ. She receives her brightness from the sun of justice, so as then to be able to say: I live, but now it is not I who live, but Christ who lives in me!" (*Hexaemeron* 4.8.32). So the church is entirely relative to Christ, entirely turned toward him and dependent on him: she grows when she announces the Word of life; she attains fullness when she celebrates the divine mysteries; and she becomes small again when she serves in the hiddenness of charity. This is the church of God, which lives by the light he gives her through the Word made flesh for us. Like Mary, the church — *oriens ex alto* — lets herself be overshadowed by the Spirit in persevering attentiveness and the contemplative receptivity of love.

In the second place, the church is given to us as a *mystery:* because she is in the first place God's handiwork, and not the product of human effort, the church in her deepest nature is inaccessible to a purely human way of looking at things. The church cannot be taken prisoner by purely worldly criteria. Even if it is true, and it will always be true, that the church is one reality among the many realities present in history, it also remains true that she is home to another Presence. She is the living memory of the One who, once having entered history, does not allow himself to be reduced to history alone. The church comes from elsewhere; whoever seeks to measure and define her by this world's criteria alone, whoever thinks to find in her just one more power among the many powers of this world, will never come to know what is truly in her heart. In the church, another world makes its appearance in this world; the Spirit enters into the flesh, deprives that flesh of its power over us, and then raises it up again to new and unimaginable life.

This meeting place between worlds, this foreign but familiar place, this intersection between a plane that is familiar to us and another, unknown yet full of power, is the church: mystery, the tent God has pitched among humankind, the fragment of flesh and time where the Spirit of the Eternal One has made his home! When, with the Bible and especially Paul, we take mystery to mean the divine plan, hidden for eternal ages but manifested in Christ Jesus and being fulfilled here and now (cf. Rom. 16:25), the eyes of our faith recognize this mystery in the church: the glory both hidden and revealed in history reveals itself to those who know how to recognize the signs of its presence with the insight born of love.

Discernment, at the personal, spiritual, and pastoral levels, implies three closely interconnected steps: accepting the complexity of the way things in fact are; measuring ourselves against the Word of God; and settling on provisional but credible ways forward. Accepting that reality is complex means recognizing the worldliness of the world in the whole interplay of historical relationships that characterize it. It means not starting one's reading of history from a preconceived ideological scheme, but setting oneself to look for the signs of the Spirit's work in the here and now. Thus accepting the world's complexity naturally brings with it the inevitable risks involved in having to deal with the ambiguities of human history. The possibility of making mistakes always lies in wait. This is why any discernment exercised in faith must always make reference to its fundamental criterion, the Word of revelation transmitted in a living way in the church. The community of believers, well versed in complexity, will not turn to the Scripture for prefabricated solutions or easy answers; they will, instead, accept that hearing this Word will often involve the patience to journey long and hard in search of understanding.

In the encounter between the Word and history — "between the Bible and the newspaper," as Karl Barth was fond of saying — faith-filled discernment will lead to proposing ways forward that are both provisional and credible. There will be no total and definitive solutions, because everything connected to history stays contingent and complex. Despite this, however, the results of this kind of discernment will enjoy a certain reliability, precisely because they issue from a twofold fidelity — to humankind and to the Word of God. Reading history in the gospel, discernment similarly reads the gospel in history; it proposes faith's point of view, not with a constantly insecure sense of anxiety, but with confidence in God's fidelity, which also speaks to today's history through the Word. It is thus we can identify the "signs of the times" (cf. Matt. 16:3), those events in which the eye of the believer perceives the unchanging and at the same time dramatic action of God in history. By the power of this divine activity the mystery of the church goes on revealing itself in all the variety of its expressions and actualizations in the days of humankind.

Finally, recalling the church's origin leads us to rethink the church as a *community involved in and committed to history:* just as the Word became flesh, entering completely into the contradictions of human existence and of death, so the church of love must become fully present in every human situation with the contagious power and peace of the Redeemer of humankind. If the God of the church entered completely into the human adventure, the church of God cannot remain on history's sidelines, holding herself aloof from the suffering and hopes of humankind. The glory of God is praised where human life is empowered: *"Gloria Dei vivens homo"* ("The glory of God is the human person fully alive"; St. Ireneus of Lyons). There is no human situation, especially of pain or of misery, to which the church may consider herself a foreigner. Her task is to be present there in a solidarity that is neither imposition nor substitution. A church where love has the first place, that walks with humankind, capable of bearing humanity's tears and protests to God, and equally capable of proclaiming the other dimension, the horizon of the Kingdom that comes, protesting against and subverting the shortsightedness of this world's calculations and presumptuousness — this is the *"Ecclesia de caritate,"* which lives by faith *"caritate formata,"* as St. Thomas Aquinas says. This is the church that sees that charity is not just one more thing to be done, but the very expression of her essence and of her deepest vocation as a people gathered by the Trinity to the glory of the God who is Love.

To reflect on the mystery of the church in this way, as flowing from the wellsprings of God's love, challenges us as disciples. In the presence of our *ecclesia mater* we ask: Do we love the church, do we really love her, recognizing in her our mother in grace, toward whom we have the greatest of all debts — the faith? Looking deep into the mystery of her coming-to-be in time according to God's plan, we ask: Do we continually discern the signs of God's presence in life and history so as to perceive the ways the Lord is calling us to build his church and help her to grow? On the individual level, this challenge involves each one of us: Do I exercise this faith-filled discernment in the context of my vocation and of the ministry to which I have been called? Do I always give the first place in everything to the contemplative dimension of life, by which the church of love is generated ever afresh? Do I recognize that I am totally relative to Christ, my Lord and my God? Do I make room in my day for the spiritual experience of the blessed Trinity, drawing life from God's Word, liturgical prayer, prolonged adoration, and works of charity? Do I try to live all my relationships in love, bearing credible witness to the church of love, of which I am a child? In particular, and as far as it depends on me, do I feel responsible for the upbuilding of the church of love, as desired by the Lord Jesus? What room do I give in my time and my heart to the love for the poorest and weakest of my traveling companions? Finally, both on the personal level and on the inseparable level of our wanting to be the church of love together, we ask in humility and truth: Are we credible in our choices and in the way we behave, so as to demonstrate that we are disciples of the Crucified Lord, who gave himself up to death for us and has poured the Spirit of God's love into our hearts? Aware of how incomplete our response has been to the demands of following Jesus as the church of love, we turn to his Father and ours with the confidence of those loved in him, who is the Beloved:

> Grant us, Father,
> to be amazed ever afresh
> by the mystery you accomplish for us in Jesus, your Son,
> and in his church, the church of love.
> Grant that we may know how to welcome this gift
> in a spirit of gratitude,
> so that your work may be accomplished for us in all things
> and your Kingdom may come.
> So grant us, we pray, to be a contemplative and eucharistic church,
> committed to praising your glory
> and serving the poor.

Let us always know how to recognize
the passing nature of all that is less than you,
so as to sing in our lives,
in communion with all our brothers and sisters in the faith,
the invincible joy of those who have believed
in the Word of your promise.
Amen. Alleluia!

14

The Church, Icon of the Trinity

We began our meditation on the church by calling to mind her origin; now we will turn our prayerful attention to the ways in which the church finds historical expression in these times between the "already" of the Lord's first coming and the "not yet" of his return.

So we ask, *What is the church in this "meantime" of salvation?* In these "penultimate" times before the last days, when Christ will hand everything over to his Father, and God will be all in all, the church thinks of herself as God's people, the community born from above and destined to journey through history back to its home on high. The church receives Christ's Spirit and so lives in communion of new life with him. Thus we can speak of the church as being the "icon" of the Trinity, molded in the image of the Trinity's own life. Just as in the Trinity's shared life (the Greek fathers called it their *perichōresis*) the three divine Persons live in one another, but without having to forgo what makes each of them distinct from the others, so in the church the multiplicity of individual persons and of local churches shares unity of life in the Spirit, and so the church becomes the one Body of Christ, yet without forfeiting the distinctiveness of the different gifts and services in their historical expression, in what is in a real way the church's own *perichōresis*.

In the light of all this, we understand why, beginning from the most ancient professions of faith, the church — the "icon of the Trinity" — has been called the *communio sanctorum*, an expression that appears in the third part of

121

the Apostles' Creed, dedicated to the Holy Spirit. The very fact that it appears in this particular place is already an indication that it contains a potentially rich reference to the third divine Person: as the *communio sanctorum*, the church shows forth the Holy Spirit at work in the people of God as they journey through history. This expression thus has various levels of meaning: touched and transformed by the one Spirit (*communio Sancti*, in communion with the Holy One), through sharing in the good things of salvation (*communio sanctorum*, communion in the holy things), and through their lives and relationships, the baptized show forth the wonderful variety of the Spirit's gifts, all directed to the common good (*communio sanctorum*, the communion among those the Spirit has made holy).

At the first level of meaning, *communio sanctorum* refers to the work of the Holy Spirit, who gives life to the church and makes her holy (*communio Sancti Spiritus*), making her into a communion of saints. Here there is a two-fold focus: on the one hand, the rich variety of gifts or charisms among the people of God, and on the other the deep union that the Comforter creates between believers from all times and places. Just as he came down on the Word made flesh, the Anointed One, the Messiah, so the Spirit comes down on each individual baptized person, enriching each with the gifts and charisms through which the one vocation to holiness finds expression in the variety of personal vocations. The church is thus wholly "charismatic," entirely pervaded by the divine Spirit's creative breath. He never ceases to call forth in her a wonderful variety of possibilities where God's love may find a home. The call is always to be open and available to these possibilities in vigilant and faith-filled discernment. Because the Spirit of Christ is one, this variety of gifts not only does not damage unity, but in fact enriches the church: "Now there are varieties of gifts, but the same Spirit; and there are varieties of services, but the same Lord. . . . In the one Spirit we were all baptized into one body — Jews or Greeks, slaves or free — and we were all made to drink of one Spirit" (1 Cor. 12:4-5, 13).

It is not only, however, at each present moment that the Spirit is at work to build up the church, the communion of saints. His activity takes in the people of God's whole journey throughout history, forging the unity of all ages in Christ, the center and Lord of time, which assures the church in every historical situation of the lasting presence in her of that which gives her life. The Spirit thus founds the historical dimension of the mystery. He is the one who ensures that the divine mysteries find expression in time; he is always alive and at work, accomplishing the wonders of salvation. It is thanks to the Spirit that the Risen Lord, once experienced by the first community, can be encountered ever anew; the Spirit makes this encounter possible, here and now, in the faith, worship, and communion of the people of God as they journey through the ages.

This, indeed, is the apostolic tradition of the church, born of the witness given by the Apostles and continuously related to that witness as its norm and foundation. This is the faithful handing on of the good things of salvation, making the community of disciples the permanent realization of the communion of the apostolic age in Christ and with him. In this sense, tradition is the history of the Spirit in the history of his church. The sign, guarantee, and privileged instrument of this tradition is the apostolic succession in the ministry. Here Christ is present as the Head of his Body the church, gathering into unity the Israel of the end times. The handing on of the ministry is thus both an expression of communion in the Holy Spirit and totally at the service of that communion. Linked especially with this is the faithful handing on of the means of salvation, the efficacious signs by which the Spirit communicates grace according to the Lord's promise. These signs — sources of the church's holiness, places of encounter with God in time — are, in different but complementary ways, the Word of God and the sacraments.

We thus come to the second level of meaning of *communio sanctorum:* communion in the holy things (the *sancta*), that is, communion in the means and gifts of salvation given by God in Christ, which form the "economy" of the sacraments *(communio sanctorum sacramentorum).* This sacramental economy is entirely relative to the Word of God, of which the sacraments are simply the highest actualization. This relationship between Word and sacrament is so close that the fathers called the Word of revelation the "audible sacrament" *(sacramentum audibile)* and the sacrament the "visible word" *(verbum visibile).* At work both in the Word of God and in the sacraments, touching our hearts and transforming them, is the same Spirit. Both in existential and in pastoral terms, we can never emphasize this relationship enough; the celebration of the sacraments should never be separated from the proclamation of the Word, which calls forth faith and makes us aware of the greatness of the gift being received; and the proclamation of the Word must never exclude the celebration of the mystery, where grace becomes an event that flows into all our human senses. This unity of the mystery proclaimed, celebrated, and lived is the full expression of the church's catholicity, of her being the fullness of that communion which shares in the divine life of the Trinity in the variety of gifts and ministries.

Then there is the third level of meaning of *communio sanctorum:* all those persons touched and transformed by the Spirit. In New Testament terms, they are the "saints" (cf., for example, Rom. 12:13; 15:26, 31; etc.). The church, generated and enlivened by the Spirit, is thus called the "communion of saints," that is, the communion of those who belong to the people gathered into the unity of the Father and the Son by the Holy Spirit. This *communio sanctorum* is above all the communion of the Lord's disciples, in the variety of charisms and ministries called forth in them by the Spirit and in their shared journey and growth.

For this communion to be achieved, a threefold "no" and a threefold "yes" are needed. The first "no" is to disengagement; no one has a right to this, because each member of the church has received gifts to be shared in service and communion. With this first "no" must go the "yes" of co-responsibility, by which all take their part in realizing the common good willed by God. The second "no" is to division; here again, no one has a right to create division, because the various gifts come from one and the same Lord and are directed to the building up of the one Body, which is the church (cf. 1 Cor. 12:4-7). With this "no" must go the "yes" to fraternal dialogue, respectful of diversity and aimed at searching constantly for the Lord's will. The third "no" is to stagnation and nostalgia; these are permitted to no one in the church, because the Spirit is always alive and at work as history unfolds. The "yes" here is to continual and necessary purification and reform, so that all the church's members may respond ever more faithfully to God's call and the whole church may fully celebrate his glory. By this threefold "no" and threefold "yes," pronounced in a dynamic and hence never entirely complete way, the church becomes the living icon of the Trinity, sharing in history in the dynamic movement of God's own life.

The one Christ and the one Spirit thus found the communion between each local church and all the others in the one Catholic church, which is the universal communion of the churches, generated by the one Word, the one Bread, and the one Spirit of the Lord Jesus. Thus, each local church recognizes itself in every other church generated by the eucharist, presided over by the bishop, and so shares in the unity of the *Catholica*, created by the one Christ, present in his Spirit, reconciling the world in himself. The individual local churches, in which and out of which the unity of the universal church is achieved, thus express in their communion a further aspect of the church's *perichōresis*: they show forth the *communio sanctorum* by cooperating, through the collegial union of their bishops under the guidance of the Bishop of the church, "who presides in love" (*prokathēmenē tēs agapēs*: St. Ignatius of Antioch, *Ad Romanos, Inscriptio*), in radiant witness to the one faith, one Lord, and one Spirit. Each bishop, as the sign and servant of the unity of his particular church, thus shares in the concern for all the churches in communion with the Bishop of Rome, who in the fullness of the *Catholica* is the sign and servant of the unity of all the Lord's disciples (*servus servorum Dei*). In the communion of the church, he proclaims the Word of the Lord, offers the sacrifice, and himself in sacrifice, for the good of all the churches, as the definitive criterion of their unity in the faith, in continuity with the ministry exercised by Peter in the apostolic college. Thus, according to the uninterrupted tradition of the Catholic faith, *communio* is full and authentic when it is lived *cum Petro et sub Petro*.

Here, too, in the relationship between the different local churches in the one church of love, a threefold "no" and a threefold "yes" are needed. Once again, the first "no" is to disengagement, because no particular church is allowed to be without a lively concern for all the others, or worse still to disassociate itself from them in some presumed independence. Here, the corresponding "yes" to co-responsibility concerns all the churches and calls for the fraternal concern of their bishops with and under Peter, in living and responsible communion in the same service to the one cause of the gospel of love. The second "no" is to division, because no church can consider itself as "everything," as if somehow alone it can show forth all the wealth of the *Catholica*. The related "yes" is to continual dialogue in communion; the passion for the visible and organic unity of the Body of Christ is part of the deepest nature of the church of love in all its expressions. Here one becomes aware of the deep scandal constituted by the division between Christians and the urgency of the ecumenical task as a duty for all, so as to achieve the unity Christ desires and in the manner he desires it, with a view to building up the unity of the whole human family according to the plan of the one Father of all. The third "no" is to stagnation and to fear of new challenges; no church can live in the past, fleeing from the present and closing itself off from the requirement of reading the "signs of the times." All the churches, in the communion of Catholic unity around the Bishop of the church who presides in love, are called to say "yes" to constant renewal as they listen to the Spirit who blows where he wills. In this sense, the worldwide communion of the church is a stimulus to perennial docility to the Lord, a school of communion for the individual local churches, and the strength to continue in the commitment to take up the ever new challenges of the times in which we are given to live, in obedience to the Truth that frees and saves.

So reflecting on the church as *communio sanctorum* stimulates us to rediscover our deepest identity as church. We can ask: How do I live out the task to which I have been called in the church and for the church, which I love? How do I shoulder responsibility and concern for the whole church, in communion with the charisms and ministries of others? How do I relate to the ministry of unity with which I am called to collaborate, and in the first place with the ministry of the successor of Peter? Am I open to the new things of the Spirit, committing myself in docile discernment to what he is saying to his people, in responsible and attentive listening to the Word of God handed on in the church, to which I owe trust and obedience? Do I faithfully nourish the life in the Spirit, offered to me by the Word of God and the sacraments? With the eyes of faith, do I recognize the church as the icon of the Trinity, in whose bosom I have been, and am continually, generated to celebrate in all things the glory of this blessed Trinity?

As we respond to these questions, and find that much still remains to be achieved, we find encouragement in the "cloud of witnesses" (Heb. 12:1), who have gone before us and who now walk with us in faith. From them, in the words of St. John Chrysostom, comes this heartfelt invitation: "Do not separate yourself from the Church! No power has its strength. Your hope is the Church. Your salvation is the Church. Your refuge is the Church. She is higher than heaven and wider than the earth. She never grows old: her youth is eternal."[2] When we love the church, St. Augustine assures us, we possess the Spirit, we meet Christ, and we live in him: "We have the Holy Spirit in the measure that we love the Church of Christ."[3] And so we ask the Lord that there may flow in us the streams of living water that gush forth from his side, the sign and fruit of our living and deep sharing in the communion of the church, the icon of the Trinity:

> Give us your Spirit,
> Lord, crucified and risen
> for love of us,
> and make us the church of love.
> Made holy by your forgiveness,
> regenerated by your grace,
> make us, Lord,
> the communion of saints,
> one in the variety of gifts and ministries,
> rich in the imagination and creativity,
> which you have entrusted to each one of us.
> Grant us to reject all disengagement,
> division, and refusal of those new things
> which you have prepared for us,
> so that in spirit and love we may live
> with a sense of co-responsibility,
> in the dialogue of communion,
> and in constant reform,
> docile to the ever-living wind
> of Pentecost.
> And in the great house of the world

2. St. John Chrysostom, *Homilia de capto Eutripio* 6.
3. St. Augustine, *In evangelium Iohannis tractatus* 32.8.

May the communion of your people,
one in the variety of times and places,
shine out as a sign and prophecy
of the future unity
promised in God who is all in all,
when you will hand all things over to the Father,
and the whole universe, reconciled in you,
will be home to the glorious Trinity.
Amen, Alleluia.

15

The Martyrdom of Peter

On this day when we are focusing our reflection on the church, one person in particular stands out among the "cloud of witnesses" (Heb. 12:1) who walk with us during this retreat. This is Peter, who is — after Jesus — the person mentioned most often in the New Testament (154 times with the name *Petros*, which means "stone" or "rock"; 27 times with the Hebrew name Simon; 9 times with the Aramaic title *Kēphas*, also meaning "rock"). These mere numerical facts already indicate the importance accorded by the early church to the role played by this apostle.

Who, then, was Simon Peter? The son of John (John 1:42) or, in Aramaic, bar-Jona, the son of Jonah (Matt. 16:17 — unless this title means that he belonged to the "barjoni" revolutionary group), Simon came from Bethsaida (John 1:44), a town on the eastern shore of the Sea of Galilee, the hometown also of Philip and, naturally, of Andrew, Simon's brother. His accent betrayed his Galilean origins. Like his brother, he was a fisherman. With the family of Zebedee, he ran a small fishing business on Lake Gennesaret (Luke 5:10: "James and John, sons of Zebedee . . . were partners with Simon"). So he was not poor; he must indeed have been financially fairly well off, and this also allowed him to cultivate his sincere religious and intellectual interests. Proof of this is the fact that he had no hesitation in accompanying his brother Andrew as far as Judea to hear the preaching of John the Baptist (cf. John 1:35-42). This also meant that he was already well disposed to respond enthusiastically to Jesus' call (cf. Luke 5:1-11).

From the Gospels we learn that Peter was married and that his mother-in-law was once cured of a fever by Jesus at Capernaum, a town situated on the northeastern shore of the lake, in the house where Simon would also stay when he was there (cf. Matt. 8:14-15; Mark 1:29ff.; Luke 4:38-39). From the Gospels, too, we learn of Simon's impulsive, at times somewhat rash, temperament; we gather this from his use of the sword, indicative of a certain familiarity with, or at least readiness to use, rather less than gentle methods (cf. John 18:10-11). At times he seems naive, even something of a showoff, and at times fearful, but nevertheless honest, to the point of being able to feel very sincere remorse (cf. Matt. 26:75) — all in all, a passionate temperament, capable of generosity, so as one day to be ready to give his life for his beloved Master.

Basing our outline on the Gospel narratives, we can identify six basic stages in Peter's spiritual journey, which was deeply marked by his encounter with Jesus of Nazareth and by the development of this relationship of faith and love, which would make of him the rock on which the Messiah was to build his church.

The first stage, a real turning point in Peter's life, can be called his *first call,* to which he responds with the energy of extraordinary trust, the expression of a faith that had learned to listen and that was open to the new things God would do:

> Once while Jesus was standing beside the lake of Gennesaret, and the crowd was pressing in on him to hear the word of God, he saw two boats there at the shore of the lake; the fishermen had gone out of them and were washing their nets. He got into one of the boats, the one belonging to Simon, and asked him to put out a little way from the shore. Then he sat down and taught the crowds from the boat. When he had finished speaking, he said to Simon, "Put out into the deep water and let down your nets for a catch." Simon answered, "Master, we have worked all night long but have caught nothing. Yet if you say so, I will let down the nets." (Luke 5:1-5)

As is evident, Jesus must have known a great deal less than Peter about fishing; and yet Simon trusts this Rabbi who does not provide him with answers but calls him to give up his life to him. His response to the miraculous catch of fish is one of awe and trepidation: "Go away from me, Lord, for I am a sinful man" (v. 8). In reply, Jesus invites him to have confidence and to go out of himself: "Do not be afraid; from now on you will be catching people" (v. 10). Peter lets himself be taken up into this great adventure; he is generous, he recognizes his limitations, he believes in the one who calls him, and he agrees to go in search of his heart's dream in Jesus' company.

Peter's second call — when, we might say, *God subverted him* — is inevitably different: Jesus is journeying with his disciples toward the villages around Caesarea Philippi, and as they walk along he puts this question to them: "Who do people say that I am?" (Mark 8:27). Their reply — "John the Baptist, and others, Elijah; and still others, one of the prophets" (v. 28) — reports the various forms of messianic expectation in Israel at the time; it is a secondhand answer and does not satisfy Jesus. He is looking for people who are willing to become personally involved, who are ready to place their very lives at risk: "But who do you say that I am?" At this point Peter, making himself the spokesperson of the group, replies: "You are the Messiah" (v. 29).

In fact, Simon has not understood all that much: he projects on to the Master the desires of his own heart, as is shown by his reaction to the way Jesus portrays his destiny as Messiah: "Then he began to teach them that the Son of Man must undergo great suffering, and be rejected by the elders, the chief priests, and the scribes, and be killed, and after three days rise again. He said all this quite openly. And Peter took him aside and began to rebuke him" (vv. 31-32). Jesus' portrayal of a suffering Messiah shocks Peter. With a certain tact, he takes it upon himself to berate the Master and to provide him with a more appropriate description of his task as Messiah, which, in Peter's eyes, cannot be reconciled with this disturbing announcement of the passion. In reality, Peter is looking for a "divine man," who will fulfill the deepest desires of his human (all too human!) heart. Jesus, completely upsetting Peter's logic, presents himself as the "human God," who, far from fulfilling Peter's dreams, subverts them. Peter is invited to recognize the outline of a great choice: to crucify Jesus on the cross of his expectations, or to crucify his expectations on the cross of

Jesus. The hard word of the Master makes all the disciple's false expectations collapse and invites him to a conversion of dream and heart: "Get behind me, Satan! For you are setting your mind not on divine things but on human things" (v. 33).

So Peter learns what it means truly to follow Jesus: "If any want to become my followers, let them deny themselves and take up their cross and follow me" (v. 34). This is indeed his second call, similar to Abraham's in Genesis 22 after his own first call in Genesis 12: it is the demanding invitation to follow the Lord. "For what will it profit them to gain the whole world and forfeit their life?" (Mark 8:36). Now, however, Peter is ready to become in some sense the new father of believers. It is no accident that Matthew places in this context the words by which Jesus entrusts to Peter his key mission as the foundation stone of his church: "And I tell you, you are Peter, and on this rock I will build my church, and the gates of Hades will not prevail against it. I will give you the keys of the kingdom of heaven, and whatever you bind on earth will be bound in heaven, and whatever you loose on earth will be loosed in heaven" (Matt. 16:18-19).

Peter learns his lesson. A sign of this is the third stage in his journey as Jesus' disciple: the *testing of his faith*. The context is Jesus' discourse on the bread of life, reported by John in chapter 6, a hard discourse to understand. Like the other disciples, Peter's faith in his Master is put to the test. Jesus certainly speaks as no one else has ever spoken, but he also says things that are frankly incomprehensible. Peter cannot but wonder in his heart how it can be possible to eat Jesus' flesh. And yet, when many of the disciples withdraw because of this difficulty and Jesus asks the Twelve, "Do you also wish to go away?" Simon Peter has no hesitation in replying, "Lord, to whom can we go? You have the words of eternal life. We have come to believe and know that you are the Holy One of God" (John 6:67-69). Certainly, Simon does not remain with Jesus because he has understood his words, but simply because they were said by Jesus and Peter believes in him. Peter's faith here is not something clear and obvious to the eyes of reason; it is a faith of abandonment to him, the Christ. This, in any case, is the fundamental law of discipleship: Jesus' call is not "see and come," as if everything must be in place beforehand and be so convincing as to produce our assent. His call is "come and see." Trusting abandonment comes before vision; the night of faith is the place where we open our heart to the dawn of God's day, whenever and however he wishes.

Peter's faith, tried and victorious in this test, is not the last word, however, as if once this challenge has been overcome we can rely on the interest we have accrued in our relationship with Christ who calls us. This is all too clear in *Peter's denials of Jesus,* in the fearful hour of Jesus' "trial." This is the fourth, and the most difficult and decisive, stage in the journey of Peter's "yes" to the Lord.

> While Peter was below in the courtyard, one of the servant-girls of the high priest came by. When she saw Peter warming himself, she stared at him and said: "You also were with Jesus, the man from Nazareth." But he denied it. . . . And he went out into the forecourt. Then the cock crowed. . . . "I do not know this man you are talking about." At that moment the cock crowed for the second time. Then Peter remembered that Jesus had said to him, "Before the cock crows twice, you will deny me three times." And he broke down and wept. (Mark 14:66-72)

As a disciple Peter has indeed followed Jesus with enthusiasm, and his faith has indeed been tested, but now he falls. Learning to believe is no triumphal procession, but a journey made of pain and love, of new testings and renewed fidelity, which only God's mercy can guarantee, renew, and keep! Peter, who had promised his Master unalloyed fidelity, now knows the bitterness and humiliation of denying him. The showoff learns humility at his own cost.

And so we come to the fifth stage in Peter's journey of discipleship, which perhaps we can call his *last confession.* Jesus' passion is now over, and the world is bathed in Easter light. Simon has gone home, to the places where the whole long journey began, and it is there, against a backdrop deeply reminiscent of his first meeting with Jesus, that the Risen One seeks Peter out, almost as if to underline that what will now take place is a new, decisive beginning in Simon's life as a disciple sent out on a mission (cf. John 21:15-19).

There is great beauty in the play of words employed in this conversation between the Risen Lord and Peter: there is *phileō,* which in Greek has to do with the love of friends, a non-exclusive love, and then there is *agapaō*, meaning unconditional, demanding, unreserved love. Jesus first asks Peter: "Simon . . . , do you love me [*agapas me*]?" (John 21:15). Before he knew what it meant to deny Jesus, Peter would certainly have replied: "I love you [*agapō se*]," but now that he has known the infinite sadness of infidelity and the drama of his own weakness, he can only bring himself to say: "*Kyrie, philō se*," that is, "Lord, I love you with my own poor love." Yet Christ insists: "Simon, do you love me?" And Peter repeats the profession of his humble love: "*Kyrie, philō se*," "Lord, I love you the only way I can." The third time, Jesus asks: "*Phileis me?*" Simon — even though saddened that it is the Lord who has now changed the verb of love — understands what this means; he understands that for Jesus this poor, humble love of his, the only love of which he now feels capable, is enough. And so he replies: "Lord, you know everything, you know that I love you [*philō se*]." And so it is Jesus who is converted to Peter, rather than Peter to Jesus! And it is this "conversion" of God that gives the disciple hope in the sorrow of his infidelity and makes him able to follow Jesus to the end: "'Someone else will fasten a belt around you and take you where you do not wish to go.' ([Jesus] said this to indicate the kind of death by which he would glorify God.) After this he said to him, 'Follow me'" (vv. 18-19). Christ's love for us founds our love for him; at his word we become able really and forever to let down the nets of our lives wherever he may lead us and haul in the catch intended and prepared by him alone.

Peter the Apostle has now reached the fulfillment of his discipleship: he has learned to own his nothingness. Now, the rock he is called to be is totally joined to the rock who is Christ, as was promised (cf. Matt. 16:18-20). Now, Peter can confirm his brothers, as Jesus had said: "I have prayed for you that your own faith may not fail; and you, when once you have turned back, strengthen your brothers" (Luke 22:32). Peter, by then well on in years, bears moving witness to his *humble love, which now overflows with joy:* as is written at the beginning of the first of the two letters that bear Peter's name, "In this you rejoice, even if now for a little while you have had to suffer various trials. . . . Although you have not seen him, you love him; and even though you do not see him now, you believe in him and rejoice with an indescribable and glorious joy, for you are receiving the outcome of your faith, the salvation of your souls" (1 Pet. 1:6-9). One can sense that the person talking here is someone who has experienced all life's trials and failures, as well as the consolations of God: "Now as an elder myself and a witness of the sufferings of Christ, as well as one who shares in the glory to be revealed, I exhort the elders among you" (5:1). Peter has learned, and points toward, the way of humility, which God loves and by which he deigns to make his way into our heart of hearts: "All of you must clothe yourselves with humility in your dealings with one another for 'God opposes the proud, but gives grace to the humble'" (5:5). Peter is truly a man of the church, bearing witness to the suffering and glorious Christ, who understands the sufferings of his brothers and how to support them in the faith, confirming them in the hour of trial as one day the Lord had confirmed and supported him.

This meditation on the martyrdom of Peter, not only the martyrdom at the end of his earthly life here on the Vatican Hill, but the whole martyrdom of the journey of his discipleship in which he learned to grow, becomes an open question for our own discernment and conversion of heart: What about us? Have we let ourselves be subverted by the Lord who calls us? Have we crucified our expectations on his cross, or have we tried to crucify him on our expectations? Are we ready to learn our nothingness and walk in faith along the way of humility, where only God is enough? Are we ready in Jesus' company to take upon ourselves our neighbor's cross, so as to offer our encouragement and support to our brothers and sisters in communion with the faith of Peter and his successors? In humility and trust we ask our Lord and Master for this grace, praying as disciples, in love and expectation:

> Lord Jesus,
> You come to us as the Living One
> who subverts and disquiets
> our plans and our defenses.
> Help us, we pray,
> not to crucify you
> on the cross of our expectations,
> but to crucify our expectations

on your cross.
Help us to let you disturb us,
so that, denying ourselves,
we may take up our cross each day
and follow you,
building up with others
the church of love.
You know that we are not capable of saying to you
the word of total love;
but we know
that our own poor love, too, is enough for you,
to make us your faithful disciples to the end.
It is this humble love we offer you:
take it, Lord,
and say again and anew
your word to us,
as one day you said it to Peter:
"Follow me."
Then, our lives will be open
to the future of your cross,
to go not where we would have wished
or dreamed or hoped,
but where you would wish
for each one of us,
in communion with our neighbor,
abandoned to you,
like true disciples, in love and expectation,
and limitless confidence.
Then, it will no longer be us
who carry the cross,
but it will be your cross carrying we,
filling our hearts with peace,
and our days with hope and love.
Amen.

16

Mary, Bride at the Messiah's Wedding-Feast: *Lectio Divina* on Luke 1:46-55

The Gospel account of Mary's visit to Elizabeth concludes with Mary's song of praise, her *Magnificat* (Luke 1:46-55). Just as the encounter between the Virgin and Elizabeth demonstrated the maternal, generous, and infectious love of the mother of the Lord, so her song of praise shows Mary to be the Bride at the Messiah's wedding feast, as she sings of how the Eternal God has now come to begin accomplishing the wonders of his love. So it is that the *Magnificat* demonstrates how the encounter between the Virgin Mother and the Trinity is in some ways a meeting of Bride and Groom; and precisely because Mary's song celebrates the new and eternal covenant established in her between the living God and his people, it is also the song of the church *par excellence*. In it, the church finds an expression of her spirituality as a covenant community and perceives that the communion she experiences is an icon of the communion that God lives. As St. Ambrose writes in his commentary on Luke: "In each one of us let it be Mary's soul that magnifies the Lord; let it be Mary's spirit that rejoices in the Lord. If according to the flesh Christ has only one mother, according to faith every soul gives birth to Christ."[4] As the song of praise sung both by Mary and the church, the *Magnificat* is truly the song of the Messiah's wedding banquet, of the covenant between earth and heaven established in the Son of Mary.

4. St. Ambrose, *Expositio Evangelii secundum Lucam* 2.26.

The Easter faith in the crucified and risen Lord is clearly expressed in the *Magnificat*. One sign of this is the way the verbs are used in the past tense (eleven are in the aorist indicative, and one in the aorist infinitive). This suggests that the Messiah's glorious manifestation has already taken place, and that the virginal conception of Jesus — recounted in Luke's Gospel only a little earlier — is a mysterious and real anticipation of what will happen at Easter:

> "He has shown strength with his arm;
>> he has scattered the proud in the thoughts of their hearts.
> He has brought down the powerful from their thrones,
>> and lifted up the lowly." (Luke 1:51-52)

Such expressions speak of the life now lived by those who have experienced the victory over death won by the risen Son of Mary.

All the same, there can be no doubt that the song originally goes back to Mary herself and that Luke has drawn on sources that predated his writing of the Gospel. Even if we leave aside the evident care with which Luke drew up his account, the fact that this song originated with Mary herself can be gathered from certain of its features that could not have seemed entirely appropriate for the person Elizabeth had greeted as "the mother of my Lord." Thus the statement that "he has looked with favor on the lowliness of his servant," which contains the word *tapeinōsis* — "low estate," "humility" — in reference to Mary (v. 48) is a clear sign that Luke adapted his text from a solid pre-Easter tradition, itself rooted in the personal experience and direct testimony of the Virgin Mother of Jesus.

Mary's song contains numerous echoes of the psalms of the poor of God (*anawim Adonai*) and, more generally, of Old Testament texts expressing longing for the Messiah to come. Thus verses 46-47 are almost a parallel of Psalm 35:9:

> Then my soul shall rejoice in the Lord,
>> exulting in his deliverance,

but also of Hannah's song in 1 Samuel 2:1-2 (cf. also Hab. 3:18):

"My heart exults in the Lord;
  my strength is exalted in my God . . .
  because I rejoice in my victory.
There is no Holy One like the Lord."

Verse 48 of the *Magnificat* seems to take up 1 Samuel 1:11, where Hannah, the future mother of the prophet Samuel, calls on the "Lord of hosts" to have consideration for "the misery of your servant" (in the Septuagint the term used is *tapeinōsis*) and to remember her (cf. also Gen. 29:32). The contrasting statements in verses 51-53 find their model in the song of Hannah in 1 Samuel 2:6-8:

"The Lord kills and brings to life;
  he brings down to Sheol and raises up.
The Lord makes poor and makes rich;
  he brings low, he also exalts.
He raises up the poor from the dust;
  he lifts the needy from the ash heap,
to make them sit with princes and inherit a seat of honor."

Verse 52 recalls Sirach 10:14:

The Lord overthrows the thrones of rulers,
  and enthrones the lowly in their place.

Verse 54 is reminiscent of Isaiah 41:8-9:

But you, Israel, my servant, . . .
you whom I took from the ends of the earth,
  and called from its farthest corners,
saying to you, "You are my servant,
  I have chosen you and not cast you off."

And verse 55, finally, recalls Micah 7:20:

You will show faithfulness to Jacob
    and unswerving loyalty to Abraham,
as you have sworn to our ancestors
    from the days of old.

The abundance of Old Testament references in the *Magnificat* is thus evident. This is a clear sign that the Virgin Mother's spirituality was rooted in the great yearning of Israel for a Messiah and deliverer. Mary was truly the Daughter of Zion, who listened in faith to the living God ("*Shema, Israel*" — "Hear, O Israel": Deut. 6:4), ever ready for his surprises. In this sense, there is no doubt that Luke placed this song on Mary's lips because, together with the original data of which he might have been in possession, he realized that these words expressed sentiments that were entirely harmonious with his understanding of Mary, which itself was founded on a nucleus of historical data on which he was able to draw because of his closeness to the life and faith of the Virgin and her Son.

What does this song tell us about the person who sang it? Presenting Mary as spokesperson for the poor in their longing for the Messiah to come, and in their joy as they see their hopes fulfilled when God acts in power at Easter, Luke portrays Mary as Christ's first disciple, for whom the hope of Israel is fulfilled and surpassed. Just as Easter was foreshadowed in the virginal conception, the words of the Virgin Mother proclaim, also as it were in advance, the good news of Jesus, and especially his predilection for the last and the least, particularly underlined by Luke (cf. Luke 7:11-17, 36-50; 10:29-37; 17:11-19). In Mary, "blessed" because she believed (cf. Luke 1:45), the new things of the gospel find exemplary fulfillment, and in her we see how God begins his new works with and from the poor. She is the Bride at the Messiah's wedding feast, and with her the Eternal One seals his new and final covenant.

What happened in this humble servant of the Most High thus becomes a reason for the poor, the sorely tried, and the suffering of the first and later Christian generations to trust and hope. Together, they will all call her blessed. The *Magnificat* is the song of salvation that can be sung by those who thought they had no right or merit in this regard; it is a celebration of the unalloyed grace that fills the heart with joy and makes the church of love a festive community gathered at the Messiah's wedding feast. Here the Bridegroom has come to fulfill the humble longing of his Bride beyond every calculation and measure. As a song of exultant joy at the coming of the Messiah, Mary's *Magnificat* is truly the song of that possible, impossible love offered by God with humanly unimaginable generosity and superabundance to all those ready to receive it in humility and faith. The spirituality of the *Magnificat* is the spirituality, too, of the church of love, born at the wedding feast of the Messiah with the people who looked forward to his coming. Mary, the Daughter of Zion, is their finest flower, and what was accomplished in her surpasses every possible human prediction. Thus the faith of the disciples finds the most beautiful confirmation of its hope and trust in the Virgin Mother's own song of faith.

Convinced of this, among many others, is a perhaps unexpected witness — Martin Luther, who, even though he bore no small responsibility for the historical division of the Body of Christ, was endowed with a "deep religious spirit, and animated by an ardent passion for the question of eternal salvation."[5] In his commentary on the *Magnificat,* the Reformer, who will also pass into history as the initiator of an anti-Marian polemic that went on to become customary in some parts of the Reformation movement, reveals toward Mary an attitude of great respect and veneration, which can also be found in other exponents of the tradition he began.

It is 1521 and, at a time of great personal danger and imminent risk, Luther turns to the Woman of the *Magnificat* to find in her the light, comfort, and help he needs. The commentary he writes on the song of the Virgin speaks of this real life situation, which impels him to seek the true reason for hope and joy — even in the hour of the most terrible testing — in the impossible possibility created by God and celebrated by the Mother of the Lord. Luther writes: "May God's sweet Mother obtain the Spirit for me, so that I can expound this song of hers fittingly and to the advantage of my readers, so that all may be able to find an understanding which will lead us to salvation and a praiseworthy life, and then to celebrate and sing this *Magnificat* eternally in heaven." Luther goes on to pray at the end of his

---

5. John Paul II in his *Letter to Cardinal Willebrands*, on the occasion of the fifth centenary of Luther's birth, November 10, 1983.

commentary: "May this song not only enlighten us and speak to us, but burn and live in our bodies and souls. May Christ grant us this by the intercession and will of his beloved mother Mary!"

The reason why the song sung by the Mother of the Lord can thus deeply enliven and enlighten the soul of Jesus' disciples and the heart of the church lies in the fact that it celebrates the joy of the Messiah's coming; it tells us where this joy originates and draws out its essential features. In the *Magnificat*, Mary sings especially of four facets of joy (four, like the points of the compass — a joy meant for all!).

The first is the joy of realizing that you are loved, that your life is lived under the loving gaze of God, your Creator and Provider. This is the *joy of living your very existence* as your response to the gift first made to you by the Creator; it is the joy described by St. Ignatius in the first part of his *contemplatio ad amorem*, the simple, pure joy of just *being*, aware of your nothingness and yet certain of being regarded and loved by the Father.[6]

Yet the joy that generates Mary's song is even more than this: it is the celebration of the good news that God-with-us has now come. This is the second facet of joy, *joy at the Messiah's coming*, the exultant joy experienced at the presence among us of the eternal Son in the womb of the Virgin Mother:

> Sing aloud, O daughter Zion;
> shout, O Israel!
> Rejoice and exult with all your heart,
> O daughter Jerusalem! . . .
> The Lord your God is in your midst,
> a warrior who gives victory. (Zeph. 3:14, 17)

This is the joy to which we are called by the angel's greeting — *Xaire* (Luke 1:28) — reminiscent of the language used by the prophets to describe the celebration of the fulfillment of the hope for the Messiah's coming (cf. also Isa. 12:6; Joel 2:21-27; Zech. 2:10; 9:9). This is the joy announced to the shepherds at Christmas: "Do not be afraid; for see — I am bringing you

---

6. St. Ignatius of Loyola, *Spiritual Exercises* 230-37.

good news of great joy for all the people: to you is born this day in the city of David a Savior, who is the Messiah, the Lord" (Luke 2:10-11). This is the joy of all who dwell in the Trinity by faith, prayer, charity, and gratitude: "If you keep my commandments, you will abide in my love, just as I have kept my Father's commandments and abide in his love. I have said these things to you so that my joy may be in you, and that your joy may be complete" (John 15:10-11).

This joy overflows and, as it were, demands to be proclaimed and shared, and this is the third facet of joy, the *joy of service*. Mary has already borne witness to this joy at the visitation, as she will indeed do throughout her life as beloved in the Beloved, up to the climactic hour of the cross and yet further, on into the mystery of Holy Saturday and the Easter of life and history: "We declare to you what we have seen and heard so that you also may have fellowship with us; and truly our fellowship is with the Father and with his Son Jesus Christ. We are writing these things so that our joy may be complete" (1 John 1:3-4). This third facet of joy comes into its own in service to others, as with Christ we bear the burden of their pain and ours, just as Mary did for Elizabeth. This is the joy of the good and faithful servant: "His master said to him, 'Well done, good and trustworthy slave; you have been trustworthy in a few things, I will put you in charge of many things; enter into the joy of your master'" (Matt. 25:21 and 23). This is the joy experienced by all who sing the *Magnificat* not just with their lips but also with their lives. Thus the church learns from Mary, the Bride at the Messiah's wedding banquet, not only to sing but also to live the wonders of the *Magnificat*, to be flooded by the joy of her Lord, and so to proclaim this joy to the very ends of the earth and to the last moment of history. As St. Ambrose said, "When the soul does something right and holy, it magnifies the divine image in whose likeness it was created, and — while it magnifies it — it exults, sharing in some way in the greatness of this image, so as to express that image in itself through the brightness of good works and the emulation of its very virtues."[7]

The fourth facet of joy celebrated in the *Magnificat* is the *joy of the last times*, savored in advance in a life lived in the Spirit: "You . . . rejoice with an

---

7. St. Ambrose, *Expositio Evangelii secundum Lucam* 2.27.

indescribable and glorious joy, for you are receiving the outcome of your faith, the salvation of your souls" (1 Pet. 1:8-9). This is the joy of the beatitudes, which draw into our human present the future of God's promise, subverting this world's logic. This is the joy of Mary, the Bride at the eternal wedding feast, blessed because she believed, an expert in the happiness proclaimed and given by her Son:

> "My soul magnifies the Lord,
> and my spirit rejoices in God my Savior,
> for he has looked with favor on the lowliness of his servant."
>
> (Luke 1:46-48)

> "Blessed are the poor in spirit, for theirs is the kingdom of heaven.
> "Blessed are those who mourn, for they will be comforted.
> "Blessed are the meek, for they will inherit the earth." (Matt 5:3-5)

So to meditate on Mary's song of praise not only fills us with hope and joy but also challenges us to evaluate our life against everything she proclaims and celebrates. We can thus ask: Are we joyful because we realize that we are the Father's beloved, living always in his sight? Do we live the infectious joy of an ever new encounter with the Lord Jesus, which is the true meaning of our lives? Do we seek to live in the Trinity by the gift of the Spirit, giving first place to the contemplative dimension of our lives, letting ourselves be filled with the love of the Three, the source of the truest and deepest joy? Do we live the joy of being servants, made such for others by the love of God in Jesus Christ? Do we work for the true joy of those entrusted to our care? How do we live out in our lives the spirit of the beatitudes and the joy of eschatological hope? Do we proclaim it and bear witness to it in word and deed?

May the Virgin Mother of the *Magnificat* help us respond to these questions with faith-filled lives, so that her song as the Bride at the Messiah's wedding feast may be our song, too, the song of hope of the beloved church of love. We make ourselves one with all generations as we confidently invoke Mary, using the words of St. Alphonsus Maria de' Liguori, who loved her and rejoiced to sing her glories:

Mother of holy Love, our life, refuge and hope, you well know that it was not enough for your Son Jesus Christ to make himself our perpetual advocate with the eternal Father, but that he also wished you to be involved with him in imploring the divine mercies for us. . . . So I turn to you, hope of the poor, myself a poor sinner. I hope, my Lady, to be saved by the merits of Jesus Christ, and then by your intercession. I have this confidence; I have it so completely, that if my eternal salvation lay in my own hands, I would place it in yours, because I trust more in your mercy and protection than in all my works. My mother and my hope, do not abandon me, as I deserve. Look upon my poverty, be moved to pity, help me and save me. . . . O Mary, I trust you; in this hope I live and in this hope I want and hope to die, with these words always on my lips: my only hope is Jesus Christ and, after Jesus, the Virgin Mary.[8]

---

8. St. Alphonsus Maria de' Liguori, *The Glories of Mary,* chap. 3, "Spes nostra, salve" ("Hail, our hope").

Fifth Day

THE CHURCH IN MISSION

On this fifth day, the journey of our spiritual exercises reaches the fulfillment of the *via unitiva*. Transformed by the Spirit of the Risen One, made sharers in the life of the Trinity, the disciples make up the church of love — called to irradiate the beauty of the Trinity in history, calling all peoples to experience the salvation that changes lives. (Developing the language of the tradition, we could say that the purpose of this day is *transformata performare* — that is, to put into practice through witness and proclamation what God has achieved in us by the gift of letting us share in the life of the Trinity.) The church journeying toward the homeland of the Trinity is the church in mission: the ship of Peter travels on the seas of time toward the harbor of the heavenly Jerusalem and guides all peoples there by the light of Christ.

So at the beginning of this day we pray the beautiful words written in 1833 by John Henry Newman on a ship between Sicily and Naples — a prayer answered beyond all measure when he entered the Catholic Church twelve years later:

> Lead, kindly Light,
> amid the encircling gloom,
> Lead thou me on!
> The night is dark,
> and I am far from home,

Lead thou me on!
Keep thou my feet!
I do not ask to see
the distant scene;
one step enough for me.

17

Journeying Home to the Trinity:
The Church in Mission

Where is the church going? Just as she comes from the Trinity and is molded in the likeness of the Trinity's shared life, so the church travels toward the Trinity as she journeys on her pilgrimage homeward through time. In the Spirit and through Christ, she journeys toward the Father; and as she presses forward toward this goal, the church experiences herself as sent forth to share the power of the reconciliation won by Christ at Easter in every historical circumstance, until he returns. The whole church is called to mission! *The whole church is sent to proclaim the whole gospel to the whole human person and to every human person.* The pilgrim church's catholicity in communion corresponds to her catholicity in mission, and this catholicity in mission concerns who in the church is sent on mission, and what they proclaim, and to whom they proclaim it.

The whole church is sent on mission: this means that, in the power of the Spirit, none of her members can be indifferent to the missionary task. The fact that the church is catholic means that *all are sent.* Even while granting the specific responsibilities that fall to the ordained ministry — discerning and coordinating the many gifts of the Spirit in the task of preaching the gospel — it remains true that every baptized person, and every local community, must use the gifts they have received in the service of the church's mission. If this certainly means that the gifts of each must be recognized and cherished, it also means that each should make an effort to grow in communion with all, in such a way that communion may become the first form mission takes: "By this everyone will know that you are my disciples, if you have love for one another" (John 13:35). Mission is not done by lone rangers but is rather to be lived out from the ship of Peter, which is another way of saying that it involves the *Catholica* in all its forms, in communion of life and action with all the baptized, each according to the gift received by the Spirit. This communion is a necessary condition for the mission of all and of each, because the many and varied gifts come from one and the same Spirit.

The catholicity of mission, however, concerns not just who goes out on mission but also what they proclaim. The intrinsic "splendor" of the saving truth requires that the church proclaim the gospel in its entirety in all the different circumstances of history. The whole church proclaims the whole gospel! The fundamental reason why the good news is thus to be proclaimed in its entirety is that the good news is not really a doctrine, but a person — Christ. He, living in the Spirit, is believed and proclaimed, and it is he, too, who sets out on mission in the persons of those who proclaim the good news. Mission calls for witness to be borne to the whole Christ: this is *the catholicity of the message,* that fullness without which the message would be adulterated and debased. When witness is borne to Christ in this complete way, the church lives in communion with all those who have believed and now believe throughout time and space. This witness gives a voice, as it were, to the communion created by the Spirit; through the apostolic tradition the Spirit keeps the church solidly planted on the foundation of her catholicity, as he mysteriously draws her into unity with her ever-present origin, Christ the reconciler proclaimed by the apostles. The catholicity of the church's message consequently requires that two opposite reductionisms be avoided, since they would render vain, in different if convergent ways, the scandalous power of the gospel: on the one hand, secular reductionism; and on the other, spiritualizing reductionism.

Secular reductionism makes an absolute of the present moment and identifies the word of faith with one or another of the powers now at play in history. The gospel witness is thus reduced to just one among the voices raised in the world; the gospel is emptied of its provocative power and becomes little more than worldly ideology, calculations, and plans, incapable of welcoming the new things done when God comes. To combat this risk, we have to emphasize the always liberating and disquieting power of the Word of God and the surprising action of the Spirit. We cannot be said to be proclaiming the gospel if we do not bear witness to new things it implies; we cannot be said truly to be loving others if we lack the courage to be different from them out of love for them and in obedience to the challenge of the living God. Christ is not a mere doctrine to let himself be manipulated according to our tastes and plans; rather, he is a person, alive with new life, who comes to us and calls us to follow him.

On the other hand, the gospel witness can be reduced in a spiritualizing way when it becomes a form of escape from history. Here the new things involved in the gift "already" received are so absolutized as to lose sight of the problems posed in the different contexts and human stories to which the gospel is proclaimed and mediated. Catholicity here is impoverished, because it is reduced to ready-made answers, without passing through the necessary mediation of interpretation, at once both faithful and creative, required by the encounter with real cultures and persons and made possible by the action of the Holy Spirit. This kind of disincarnate spiritualism, we might say, knows how to say the various kinds of no involved in the gospel, but it often neglects the different kinds of yes, even if sometimes humble and provisional, which all of us need to say if we want to be able to live and to die as truly human beings. The God of the gospel is not like that. He does not make impossible demands; he is the God-with-us, who "worked with human hands, thought with a human mind, acted with a human will, loved with a human heart," and precisely in this way, "revealing the mystery of the Father and His love, also revealed human beings to themselves and made known to them their high calling" (*Gaudium et Spes,* 22). To counter the danger of all kinds of spiritualizing escapism, the church must walk with all the human beings to whom she proclaims the gospel. Human beings are the path the church must walk!

The catholicity of the message also implies the catholicity of those to whom this message is addressed: the good news has sounded out for all and must reach all. The "splendor" of the truth offers itself by emptying itself into the most varied languages and cultures. "Go . . . and make disciples of all nations, baptizing them in the name of the Father and of the Son and of the Holy Spirit, and teaching them to obey everything I have commanded you" (Matt. 28:19-20). It is precisely in missionary outreach to the whole human being in every human being that Christ guarantees his faithful presence among his people: "Remember, I am with you always, to the end of the age" (v. 20). Christ is to be found wherever his witnesses proclaim his paschal mystery and wherever the church makes that mystery present and calls people to follow him. The frontier of evangelization is thus not an externally recognizable demarcation line between sacred and profane space, but above all the space of the saving decision, the human heart, where the whole of a life touched by the Holy Spirit decides for Christ or shuts itself against him. In this sense, we can also say that the church evangelizes only if she herself is continually being evangelized, letting herself be purified and renewed by the judgment of the Word of God and by the fire of the Spirit, in the down-to-earth reality of her journey through history and of the positions she has to take along the way; thus she stands *sub Verbo Dei* and can trustingly celebrate the divine mysteries for the salvation of the world.

The catholicity of mission is not yet, however, fully accomplished if the church does not at the same time open herself up to the multiplicity of human needs and to the fact that the gospel must be proclaimed to every creature. It is here that we find the unavoidable demand for every baptized person, as well as every particular church and the universal church, to be committed to proclaiming the gospel to every human being; no space or dimension of history can be left without this message. While the Lord will not ask his disciples for an account of who has been saved, because salvation is a mystery of grace and freedom that no one can determine from outside, he will certainly ask them for an account of those to whom the gospel has been preached. In this sense, a church without a sense of missionary urgency and passion would betray her catholicity and would be more a cemetery than the community of the risen in the Risen.

As the whole church — the *Ecclesia viatorum* — continues her journey homeward, her entire life is marked by the power of mission. Above all, from the conviction of being permanently sent out to proclaim the gospel the church derives an *awareness of her own relativity*. No gain, no success must ever temper the ardor with which she awaits her Lord's coming; every thought of having somehow "arrived," every "ecstasy of achievement," is a temptation and a brake. The church of love is not yet the Kingdom in glory, but only the Kingdom that has begun, *"praesens in mysterio"* (*Lumen Gentium*, 3). She carries in herself the passing nature of this world and, *semper reformanda*, she knows she is called to unceasing renewal and continual purification, neither quenched nor quenchable by any human victory, tending "unceasingly towards the fullness of divine truth, so that the words of God may find fulfillment in her" (*Dei Verbum*, 8). Nothing could be further from the style of a missionary church, docile to the Spirit at work in history, than an attitude of giving in to the seductive power of the present moment and of worldly possessions.

The fact that the church lives out her call in this eschatological way means that she also *ascribes only a relative value to the great things of this world.* Present as she is in every human situation, in solidarity with the poor and oppressed, it will never be right for her to identify her final hope with any of the penultimate hopes offered by history. This critical vigilance does not, however, mean disengagement; it is, on the contrary, costly and demanding. It means that the church takes to herself the hopes of the men and women of her time and tests them against the Lord's resurrection, which on the one hand sustains every authentic commitment to liberation and human promotion, while on the other it challenges every attempt to make human goals absolute. In the name of this "eschatological reservation" of hers, the church's mission cannot be identified with any ideology, party, or system, but must be the critical conscience of all of these, calling men and women to recognize their first origin and last goal, acting as a stimulus for the promotion of the whole human being in every human being. The homeland that makes Christians strangers and pilgrims in this world is not a dream alienating them from reality, but a power impelling them to commit themselves to justice, peace, and the integrity of creation in today's world.

Finally, the call to journey homeward fills the church with hope and joy. The fact that she looks forward in this particular way makes her able *to act even now,* in the power of the Spirit, to effect victory over suffering, evil, and death. Despite the trials and contradictions of these present times, the people of God already exult in the hope that the divine promise has lit in the heart of her faith. Sustained by this hope, this sure guarantee that history's last word will not be suffering, sin, and death, but joy, grace, and life, the church presses toward the goal, which already fills her with exultant joy. The words of the psalm come true in her: "I was glad when they said to me, 'Let us go to the house of the Lord!'" (Ps. 122:1). To believers there remains the task of living the mystery of Advent at the heart of human life: "The Spirit and the bride say, 'Come.' . . . The one who testifies to these things says, 'Surely I am coming soon'" (Rev. 22:17, 20). It is of this desire, of this joyful expectation, that the church's mission speaks in the most varied times and places of history.

Thinking in this way about the missionary nature of the whole church in her journey toward the glory of the Trinity generates some demanding questions that every disciple of the Lord Jesus is challenged to answer: Do I give myself unstintingly to serve the mission entrusted by Christ to his people? Do I live out my particular mission in responsible communion with all the members of the church in the variety of our gifts? Do I proclaim the whole gospel, without giving in to secularizing reductionism or escapist spiritualization? Do I try to reach the whole human being in every one of the human beings to whom I am sent by virtue of the mission entrusted to me? Do I try to live in a constant state of being renewed by the breath of the Spirit, giving my support to the continual renewal of the whole church? Am I always vigilant of the ever-present risk of letting myself be seduced by the ways of worldly power or this world's great things? Above all, do I seek, and bear witness to, the joy and peace experienced by all those who see themselves as pilgrims journeying homeward? Do I always walk in this direction, strengthened by the Spirit encountered in the fraternal communion of the church?

In the church entirely given to mission, the mystery of revelation and hiddenness continues to become present. It is of this mystery that Lady Church sings as she is sent forth to bear witness in the sight of all to that victory in which death has been and will be slain, the victory she has seen accomplished in the gardener of God's new garden, in the Word crucified and risen to live, Jesus Christ, true light of the world:

Christ the Lord is ris'n today;
Christians, haste your vows to pay;

Offer you your praises meet
At the Paschal Victim's feet.
For the sheep the Lamb has bled,
Sinless in the sinner's stead;
Christ, the Lord, is ris'n on high,
Now he lives no more to die.

Christ, the Victim undefiled,
Man to God has reconciled;
When in strange and awful strife
Met together death and life;
Christians, on this happy day
Haste with joy your vows to pay.
Christ, the Lord, is ris'n on high,
Now he lives no more to die.

Christ, who once for sinners bled,
Now the firstborn from the dead,
Throned in endless might and power,
Lives and reigns forevermore.
Hail, eternal Hope on high!
Hail, our King of Victory!
Hail, our Prince of life adored!
Help and save us, gracious Lord![1]

1. Easter sequence, ascribed to Wipo of Burgundy, eleventh century (trans. Jane E. Leeson).

18

Eucharist and Beauty

A wonderful passage in the writings of St. Augustine introduces us to the theme of this present meditation, by summarizing in a particularly intense way what we have been contemplating about the church and Christ, the church's Head and Lord, whom the Gospel of John (10:11) portrays as "the beautiful Shepherd":

> Two flutes play different tunes, but the same Spirit breathes through them both. The first: "You are the most handsome of men" [Ps. 45:2]; and the second: "He had no form or majesty that we should look at him" [Isa. 53:2]. One and the same Spirit plays the two flutes: so they play in harmony. Do not fail to listen to them, but try to understand them. Let us ask the apostle Paul to explain the perfect harmony between the two flutes. Let the first play: "the most handsome of men," "though he was in the form of God, he did not regard equality with God as something to be grasped" [Phil. 2:6]. This is how the beauty of the sons of men is surpassed. Let the second play: "that we should look at him," he who "emptied himself, taking the form of a slave, being born in human likeness" [Phil. 2:7]. "He had no form or majesty" so that he might give you beauty and form. What beauty? What form? The love of charity, so that you may run in love, and love with the energy of one who runs. . . . Look to Him through whom you have been made beautiful.[2]

2. St. Augustine, *Homilies on the First Epistle of John*, homily 9.

The love with which he has loved us transfigures the "man of suffering . . . acquainted with infirmity . . . from whom others hide their faces" (Isa. 53:3) into "the most handsome of men": crucified love is the beauty that saves.

St. Thomas Aquinas takes the paradox of this beauty further: when he comes to consider the beautiful, he speaks of the Son. In Thomas's view, beauty is an especially appropriate way of talking about the Son because beauty has three features that are also present in him: integrity, form, and splendor. Beauty, indeed, happens when the All makes itself present in the fragment; it happens, too, in the right proportion of the "form," capable of reproducing the harmony of the whole "on a small scale" (thus it is that *formosus* means beautiful!); and finally, beauty happens like a burst of light when Beauty breaks into our reality and evokes ecstatic delight in us.[3]

In the Son Jesus, all these three expressions of beauty meet. Because he is the image of the invisible God, he renders God's face or form present in human flesh; because in him infinite Love breaks into death, he redeems our finitude by entering into it as light into darkness. Here Greek thought — for which beauty is *forma,* the this-worldly reproduction of the "heavenly numbers" — encounters what is new in Christian faith, which contemplates beauty in the One before whom we cover our faces, in the infinitely Good who handed himself over for us into the finitude of abandonment. In the Son, the Whole dwells in the fragment, the Infinite breaks into the finite: the Crucified God is the form and splendor of eternity in time. On the cross, the *Verbum abbreviatum* — *kenosis* or self-emptying of the eternal Word — reveals the Beauty that saves!

This mystery of the Son's beauty is consigned to all at the Last Supper, the memorial in which by the Spirit's power the event of Calvary is represented in time. In the fragment of the Eucharistic signs there is the whole of him who is Love in person, crucified and risen to give himself. The Eucharist is the sacrament in which the eternal becomes present in time, the Trinity is here in history, and the history of the Trinity is welcomed and received. Precisely because of this, in the Eucharist is found the beauty that saves. Because, then, the church is born from the Eucharist, the *sacramentum unitatis*, the beauty that offers itself in this sacrament is passed

---

3. Thomas Aquinas, *Summa Theologica* I q. 39 a. 8 c.

on to the whole communion of saints. This movement from beauty to beauty — from the beautiful Shepherd to the sacramental beauty of the Eucharist and on to the church's beauty — causes the light of the divine Sun to shine in the night of our time; the church that celebrates the Eucharist is like the full moon, radiantly beautiful with the beauty of Christ, her Bridegroom. Thus the three inseparable aspects of the Eucharistic celebration — "paschal memorial," "sacrificial banquet," and "pledge of future glory" — are like three windows opening on to the one Beauty that saves, offered to human beings in the fragments of the bread of life and the chalice of salvation.

The first aspect of the Eucharist is that it is the *paschal memorial*, celebrated by the church obedient to the Lord's command, in "memory" of him (cf. Luke 22:19 and 1 Cor. 11:24-25). In the biblical tradition, "memorial" here is not the mere calling to mind of a past event, similar to the Western idea of "remembrance," meaning a purely conceptual movement from the present to the past by a kind of dilation of the mind (*extensio animi ad praeterita*). It is rather a movement in quite the opposite direction, from the past to the "today" of the Eucharistic celebration itself. The Hebrew terms *zikkaron, azkarah,* translated into Greek by *anamnēsis, mnēmosynon,* express the becoming present here and now by God's power of the unique and definitive event of salvation. The "already" of the Passover of the Lord is represented in the celebration of the people of God journeying in time, in order to make effective here and now the reconciliation that saves. And just as in the paschal event it is the Trinity that is at work, so in the Eucharistic memorial it is the Trinity's work that becomes present: the church calls on the Father, "holy and fountain of all holiness," so that he may send the Spirit on the gifts of bread and wine and make sacramentally present in them the suffering and glorified Christ. By partaking of these holy gifts, the church knows she is being built up into "one body and one spirit." In the Eucharist the church thus celebrates the powerful memorial of her origin, the Trinity's initiative of love that has placed her in time as a sign and instrument of unity for all humankind.

The Eucharist is a meeting place with beauty above all for the celebrating priest through the uninterrupted continuity of the apostolic succession. He is bound by the sacrament of ordination to the one high and eternal Priest, who on the night of the Last Supper entrusted to his apostles and their successors the command of celebrating in memory of him for the salvation of the world. It is this rootedness in the apostolic tradition that makes the ordained minister an *alter Christus,* one who acts *in persona Christi.* Presiding at the celebration of the Eucharistic memorial is not simply a matter of performing a "function," but has its roots in *being,* the mystery by which the ordained minister is sacramentally configured to the "beautiful Shepherd," Christ the priest, "so that he can act in the person of Christ the head" of the body, the church.[4]

This is why the priest — by virtue of his very condition as the one who presides over the Eucharist — is called to place himself, in the first place and in an exemplary manner, in an attitude of receptivity to the gift of God, through a spirit of gratitude and the contemplative depth of his own life. In this sense, "to preside" means above all "to receive," to let oneself be flooded with the beauty of Christ in order to irradiate this to all. Together with the priest as he acts *in persona Christi Capitis,* the whole community over which he presides in the Eucharistic celebration is called to welcome the gift. Here we find the roots of the Christian vocation to be persons of prayer, expert listeners, ready to welcome the gifts of the Spirit, "Eucharistic persons" in the entirety of our being and doing, committed at one and the same time to discern and bear witness to the signs of God's beauty in the life of the church and the world.

While the baptismal and ministerial priesthood come to exist by receiving the gift from on high, they no less exist by giving that gift: by celebrating the Eucharist, Jesus' disciples are led to share the same condition in which Jesus placed himself at the Last Supper. The Old Testament references in the Gospel accounts of the institution of the Eucharist agree in delineating the figure of Christ as that of the Suffering Servant (cf. Isa. 42:6; 49:8-9); and, while they make use of the sacrificial image of the lamb (cf. 53:7), they also teach that sins were expiated through the substitution of an innocent victim for sinners (cf. 53:10-12; Matt. 26:28; Mark 14:24). The influence of the figure of the Suffering Servant on the description of the Last Supper is confirmed by the evangelist Luke, who in the context of

4. Pope Paul VI, *Presbyterorum Ordinis,* 2.

the Supper reports two of Jesus' sayings regarding the service to be offered by those who have authority (Luke 22:24-27), as well as by John, who sees in the washing of the feet the perfect expression of the inner meaning of the Eucharist, of which he does not speak (cf. John 13:1-20).

The link between the Servant and the Supper is thus not accidental but is part of the very meaning of the Eucharistic memorial. The church, which in this memorial finds its life and truest expression, must then share in the fate of the Servant, becoming herself a servant. Eating the bread that is given, she must become, by the power that bread gives her, a church whose body is given, a body for others, a body offered for the many. The beauty that saves and that makes itself present in the Eucharist finds particularly eloquent expression in the gift of a life offered day by day out of love. It is not by chance that in the early church the term "charity" (agapē), by which the Good Shepherd draws close to his own, was taken to mean both the memorial of the Lord's Supper and the fraternal community that it generated and expressed.

The Eucharist as memorial is inseparably bound to the second aspect of this sacrament: the Eucharist as *sacrificial banquet*. The early church bears clear testimony to having understood this indivisible unity: "As often as you eat this bread and drink this cup, you proclaim the Lord's death until he comes" (1 Cor. 11:26). Already at the very level of the signs involved in this sacrament, the bread of the Supper is the bread of fraternity, and the chalice of wine indicates how those who drink it come to share in the same destiny. In the Jewish tradition, to share table-fellowship is to share life itself, and the chalice stands for the suffering to which each is destined. The breaking of the bread, with the distribution of a small piece to each of those present, as well as the partaking in the same chalice are signs of a deep solidarity, a shared destiny.

Jesus thus explicitly links the institution of the Eucharist to a banquet shared by brothers and sisters: in this way he makes it evident — through the signs he chooses and the context in which he celebrates — that the paschal memorial intimately concerns the church. It follows that the celebration of this memorial of his Passover both requires and founds the communion of those gathered in Christ and among themselves: the communion in the holy gifts (*communio sanctorum*) produces the communion of saints (also *communio sanctorum*!). This *communio* will above all find expression in the relationship between each of the baptized and their bishop, and between them and both the local church and the *Catholica*, this latter presided over and signified by the Bishop of the Church who presides in love. This communion — even though at times it may be hardwon and painful — is the sign of the beauty of the God who makes one the hearts of those who have had a deep experience of this beauty. Such beauty can really be good news in a world that — especially in this postmodern age — often seems like a multitude of solitudes!

Finally, at the Last Supper Jesus announces that he will not drink of the fruit of the vine until the day when he drinks it with his own in his Father's Kingdom (cf. Matt. 26:29; Mark 14:25) — that is, until his Kingdom comes (cf. Luke 22:18). Eating the bread and drinking the chalice of the Eucharist, the disciples announce the death of the Lord until he returns (cf. 1 Cor. 11:26). The banquet of the new Passover urges us on toward another banquet, the definitive banquet of the Kingdom: the Eucharist now is the anticipation and promise of this supreme banquet and empowers history to move in its direction. The memorial that Jesus entrusts to his apostles is the pledge of future glory, *panis viatorum*, the bread of pilgrims and the nourishment of a hope that does not disappoint. In this sense, the Eucharist is the sacrament of the world's hope, anticipation of that beauty which does not fade and which has been promised to the whole of creation!

The third aspect of the Eucharist, as *the pledge of future glory*, thus marks the life of the disciples in a number of ways. In the first place, because the Eucharistic banquet always empowers the "already" to grow toward the "not yet," it implies in whoever celebrates it a deep and continuous purification and unceasing renewal. In this regard, St. Bernard has no hesitation in remarking: "The bitterness of the Church is bitter enough when the Church is persecuted by tyrants; it is even more bitter when the Church is divided by heretics; but it is most bitter of all when the Church is tranquil and at peace."[5] The *panis viatorum* sets the church continually on her way, freeing her from the illusion of already having arrived *in patria*, in that fulfillment of

---

5. *Sermones super Cantica Canticorum* 33.16: *"Amaritudo Ecclesiae sub tyrannis est amara; sub haereticis est amarior; sed in pace est amarissima."*

the promised heavenly Jerusalem reserved to the time when the Beautiful Shepherd will return in glory and will fill her with joy and hope. Inasmuch as the Eucharist is *viaticum*, food that provides stamina for the journey, the Eucharistic banquet sustains the exodus of the present time and fills it with the light of God's promise. The bread of pilgrims is the bread of hope (*pharmakon athanasias* — "medicine of immortality," the Greek fathers would say), a bread that makes the disciples free in faith from all this world's greatness, servants for love's sake, and, even when tested, witnesses to the hope that has been given in the Christ risen from the dead; thus it is that in the life of Christians, too, beauty's two flutes, of which St. Augustine speaks, play in unison, and the disciples, led by the Spirit who blows in them, can truly "run in love, and love with the energy of one who runs."

Examining our lives against the perspectives opened up by the relationship between Eucharist and beauty now becomes a question and a prayer: In the Eucharist, and beginning from the Eucharist, do I give first place in my life to the contemplative dimension? If I am a priest, do I exercise my ministry as one who presides over the Eucharist as a form of "receiving," which expresses itself in the uninterrupted gratitude of my life? Do I commit myself to learn from the mystery of faith, which is the Eucharist, to live in the recognition of the beauty of God, wherever this is revealed or hidden? Do I express the richness of the gift received in the paschal memorial through the charity of my actions? Do I live in the communion of which the Eucharist is both school and source? Do I draw from this sacrament of the encounter with Christ, missionary of the Father, the energy and fidelity to commit myself to mission? Do I feel impelled by the Eucharistic celebration to commit myself to a continual reform of my life, and to critical vigilance whenever one or another form of worldliness seems to be making some absolute claim on me? Am I a witness to the hope and joy that come from the Eucharist to my heart and life?

Aware of our fragility, we turn with confidence to him who in the bread of life continually offers us the beauty of his gift, the help and pledge of a true and full life:

We give you thanks, Lord Jesus Christ,
because you desired to entrust to your church

the memorial of your Passover.
Grant us the grace of celebrating in our lives and histories
the powerful memory of your passion
and of your resurrection
by the gift of the Spirit,
who fulfills your holy promise in history.
Grant that, docile to him,
we may know how to let ourselves be transformed by this promise,
and, united in him
by the mystery of your body and your blood,
we may know how to live and grow in communion
so that all we do may speak of the church
according to the mission you entrust to each one of us.
And may the holy banquet of this present day
be for us the living and delightful pledge
of the banquet in which we will eat forever
the bread of the Kingdom.
Amen! Alleluia!

19

Paul, Proclaiming the Good News

On this day of our retreat when we are focusing especially on mission, we choose — from among the "cloud of witnesses" (Heb. 12:1) who are walking with us — Paul, the apostle of Jesus Christ, model of those who proclaim the Good News. Throughout his entire apostolic mission, Paul was, and desired to be nothing other than, a humble disciple of Jesus, the imitator of his Lord (1 Cor. 11:1), his servant and apostle (Rom. 1:1). To come to know Paul, then, is to come to know Christ. St. John Chrysostom rightly stated that he owed all his knowledge as a theologian, pastor, and disciple of Christ to his love for Paul and to the fact that every week he faithfully read the fourteen letters (including Hebrews, which he attributed to Paul)!

What we know of Paul comes above all from the book of the Acts of the Apostles (written by Luke at the beginning of the 60s AD), almost entirely given over to the story of Paul's call and missionary journeys. The Letters, too, contain important biographical information. Paul was born at the beginning of the Christian era, so that in the account of the stoning of Stephen, at which he was present, he is described as a young man (Acts 7:58). He was born in Tarsus in Cilicia, "an important city," as he himself says (Acts 21:39). He came from a Jewish family that was well enough off to be able to acquire Roman citizenship. His parents, who must in all likelihood have very much wanted this child, called him Saul, "the desired one"; he was called Paul, the name used from Acts 13:9 onward, perhaps in memory of the proconsul Sergius Paulus whom Paul converted while in Cyprus.

At Tarsus he learned to speak Greek fluently, but he was brought up in the Jewish tradition; his parents took a lively interest in his education and sent him to Jerusalem when he was about thirteen or fourteen years old to study under Gamaliel, one of the most illustrious teachers of the Torah of the time. Having presumably returned to Tarsus, he had no opportunity of meeting Jesus personally. He learned the art of making travelers' tents, much in demand in a trading crossroads like Tarsus. Very soon, however, the humdrum existence that seemed to await him left him unsatisfied. Probably against his parents' inclination, he decided to return to Jerusalem, where he joined the Pharisee party, and as a fervent Pharisee he threw himself into the battle against early Christianity. He took part in the condemnation of Stephen. He was a cultured, fiery young man, ardent in his Jewish faith, endowed with a practical spirit and the ability to take decisions.

Around AD 35-36, in the full flood of his anti-Christian fervor, he was on the way to Damascus where he was intending to play his part in halting the evangelizing work of the disciples of Jesus the Christ, when an event took place that was to transform his life. This was no mere moral conversion or change of mind. The event — described in the third person in Acts 9 and autobiographically in Acts 22 and 26 — was the experience of an encounter, an encounter with Christ who led Paul to see everything in a new way. He understood that the faith he planned to persecute did not consist above all in a doctrine, but in a person, Jesus the Christ, the Living One, who took the initiative of revealing himself to him: "I am grateful to Christ Jesus our Lord, who has strengthened me, because he judged me faithful and appointed me to his service, even though I was formerly a blasphemer, a persecutor, and a man of violence" (1 Tim. 1:12-13). Referring to what had happened, Paul spoke of a revelation and of a mission (cf. Gal. 1:15-16), as well as of an apparition (cf. 1 Cor. 15:8-9). Because of his upbringing, his studies, and his temperament, Paul had thought he possessed God and considered himself righteous; now he discovered that he had instead been touched and possessed by God, justified by him alone: "If anyone else has reason to be confident in the flesh, I have more: circumcised on the eighth day, a member of the people of Israel, of the tribe of Benjamin, a Hebrew born of Hebrews; as to the law, a Pharisee; as to zeal, a persecutor of the church; as to righteousness under the law, blameless. Yet whatever gains I had, these I have come to regard as loss, because of Christ" (Phil. 3:4-7). His previous certainties had been turned completely upside down; now Paul accepted that he no longer belonged to himself, but to Christ, and he let Christ lead him wherever he wished.

This first, overwhelming beginning was followed by times of silence, and then of the first enthusiasms and of testing. At the start, for Paul to answer the call meant a process of detachment, an experience of real darkness and blindness (cf. Acts 9:8-9; 22:11, 13). The light that enveloped Saul/Paul led him to perceive the whole burden of personal sin and of rootedness in sin that weighs heavily on the human condition; he spoke of this with unrivalled eloquence, for example, in his letter to the Romans (chap. 7), where he describes the tragic condition of human beings, their powerlessness to do the right thing despite their best intentions. The Lord led him to understand how much he would have to suffer for his name (Acts 9:16). While this process of inward growth was still going on, he began to proclaim Christ with enthusiasm. He did this first in Damascus itself, but the hatred of the Jews very soon compelled him to flee in what can only be described as a somewhat picturesque manner (cf. Acts 9:23-25). He returned to Jerusalem, but there many of the disciples feared him, not yet believing that he had truly become a disciple (Acts 9:26). Barnabas trusted him and took him into his company, helping Paul to find acceptance also among the others; thus was born a friendship that was one of the most beautiful gifts of Paul's life.

Despite Barnabas's efforts, however, Paul in the end was forced to leave Jerusalem, too, at the unfeigned insistence of his own brethren in the faith, who were fearful that his evangelizing ardor might provoke an even more bitter persecution than that already under way (cf. Acts 9:27-30). Saul, confused and humiliated, returned to Tarsus. He remained there for several years (at least until AD 43), in a gray existence all the harder to bear because he had fled it earlier when he was young and now felt that it was even more urgent to escape it again. So the days of his first enthusiasm were followed by bitterness and disappointment: not only the adversaries of Christianity misunderstood him, but also his own brothers in the faith. He became familiar with loneliness, a sense of shame toward his family, a feeling that his dreams had been vanquished, and the humanly inevitable sadness of not achieving his mission, an achievement that now seemed impossible.

It was Barnabas, his very dear friend, who was to lead him out of this time of testing and launch him on the way to his great missionary work. From the accounts in Acts Barnabas appears to have been a wise, balanced, prudent, and at the same time generous man, able to understand and make the most of the volcanic Paul. Showing an initiative as audacious as it was free, he went to Tarsus to fetch Paul and brought him with him to Antioch, where there was a community that wanted his help, because the mission was flourishing far beyond their wildest expectations, and the disciples — who were called "Christians" here for the first time — needed assistance in preaching the gospel. Barnabas and Paul set to work together, and everything seemed to be proceeding wonderfully. At first in Acts (chapters 11 and 13–15) Barnabas's name is mentioned before Paul's; later the contrary is the case. The two friends were, in fact, very different: Paul was as volcanic as Barnabas was balanced and diplomatic (even regarding Judaism, with which he was ready to make compromises; cf. Gal. 2:13). Thus came what was perhaps the most painful moment in Paul's life: his break with Barnabas. The circumstances had to do with a young disciple, John Mark (Mark the evangelist?), who proved to be less than enthusiastic during the first missionary journey, to the point of wanting to return home (cf. Acts 13:13). This was enough to make Paul not want John Mark with him anymore. (He would later "rediscover" John Mark and have him sent for, so as to benefit from his care and help: "Get Mark and bring him with you, for he is useful in my ministry": 2 Tim. 4:11!) Barnabas, in contrast, did not want to lose anyone and felt that the young man should be given another chance (cf. Acts 15:37-40). Paul and Barnabas — both in love with the Lord, but totally different — decided to part ways because of their different view of a question that each of them thought he had judged with the eyes of truth and love! Holiness — as may be observed — does not abolish temperament; and, in hindsight, it would seem that Barnabas had been right.

Then followed Paul's great missionary journeys, with countless trials and consolations:

Five times I have received from the Jews the forty lashes minus one. Three times I was beaten with rods. Once I received a stoning. Three times I was shipwrecked; for a night and a day I was adrift at sea; on frequent journeys, in danger from rivers, danger from bandits, danger from my own people, danger from the Gentiles, danger in the city, danger in the wilderness, danger at sea, danger from false brothers and sisters; in toil and hardship, through many a sleepless night, hungry and thirsty, often without food, cold and naked. I am under daily pressure because of my anxiety for all the churches. (2 Cor. 11:24-28)

Through all these experiences, held together by his love for Christ and by the power of Christ's grace, a kind of transfiguration took place in Paul. Especially powerful and moving evidence for this is provided by the speech he made at Miletus, reported in chapter 20 of Acts. It is a farewell, one could almost say Paul's last will and testament, and in a certain fashion sums up his whole life. The opening is touching: "You yourselves know . . . ," Paul begins, meaning that the facts will speak for themselves: he had given himself totally to his ministry, with immense love for Christ and Christ's own, with deep humility toward others, himself, and God (cf. Acts 20:18-35).

Paul was a man who knew what it meant to be put to the test, and he stood faithful to the end, because he had himself experienced the faithfulness of God in Jesus Christ: "To keep me from being too elated, a thorn was given me in the flesh, a messenger of Satan to torment me, to keep me from being too elated. Three times I appealed to the Lord about this, that it would leave me, but he said to me, 'My grace is sufficient for you, for power is made perfect in weakness'" (2 Cor. 12:7-9). Truly, Christ had transfigured him (indeed, the very description of his conversion in Acts has similarities with the transfiguration of Jesus in Luke 9), and Paul held this experience dear, learning to empty himself totally of himself, to be full only of God, and thus to give himself to others as a person truly in love with his Lord: "I have been crucified with Christ; and it is no longer I who live, but it is Christ who lives in me. And the life I now live in the flesh I live by faith in the Son of God, who loved me and gave himself for me" (Gal. 2:19-20). Thus he had no hesitation in calling himself "a prisoner of Christ

Jesus" (Eph. 3:1; cf. also 4:1), a "servant of Jesus Christ, called to be an apostle, set apart for the gospel of God" (Rom. 1:1). In Christ he worked with others for their joy (cf. 2 Cor. 1:24); he was a demanding witness and at the same time a loving father (cf. 1 Cor. 4:14-16). He was ready to follow his Master along the way of the cross to the end.

The cross was, indeed, the fate that awaited him: completing in his own flesh what was lacking in the passion of Christ for the benefit of his body, the church, Paul experienced for himself the passion of his Lord, going to meet his death with living faith and generous love. "I am now rejoicing in my sufferings for your sake, and in my flesh I am completing what is lacking in Christ's afflictions for the sake of his body, that is, the church" (Col. 1:24). Chapters 21–28 of Acts have been called the *passio Pauli*: this is the passion of the disciple, his journey in captivity, which ended with his martyrdom during the persecution under Nero (64-65). Paul was beheaded by the sword at the third milestone on the Via Ostiense in the place called Aquae Salviae, and he was buried where the Basilica of St. Paul-Outside-the-Walls stands today. According to a very beautiful tradition, when his head fell from his body it bounced three times, causing three fountains to spring up, the image of the living water, which, proclaimed by the apostle and by the gospel, would continue to flow through history to the very ends of the earth and until the last moment of time. The similarities with the passion of Christ are many: like Jesus, Paul was arrested while in the midst of his mission (cf. Acts 21); like Jesus, Paul was left alone (cf. 2 Tim. 4:9-18); he always had with him, however, the One who gave him strength: "For this I toil and struggle with all the energy that he powerfully inspires within me" (Col. 1:29). Differently from Jesus, Paul defended himself in various speeches, but he did this above all to have the opportunity of proclaiming Christ. He thus completed in himself the passion of the Messiah, to whom he gave himself with all his heart, and like his Lord he offered his life for the church, sealing his love in the eloquent silence of martyrdom. The great preacher of the gospel concluded his earthly life speaking from the tallest and sturdiest of pulpits, the pulpit of martyrdom.

In the presence of Paul's faith, his witness of love, and the passion with which he unstintingly proclaimed the gospel both in season and out of season, we cannot but find ourselves asking many questions, and evaluating our lives and hearts about our task as servants and proclaimers of Christ's gospel. The fundamental question is the one that Paul evokes in everyone by his life spent totally for the Lord, who really was his all: Who is Christ for me? Is he, as for Paul, the Living One whom I have encountered, to whom I belong, and whose prisoner I desire to be in freedom and love? Do I live in Christ, and for him, and with him? Certainly, Paul's character had its limitations. This too, however, can be of help to us, because it leads us to ask in humility and truth, Do I recognize the limitations of my character and of others, and do I accept them, making every effort to let myself be transfigured by Christ in the service of the gospel? Paul did not spare himself for the gospel. What meaning do we find for ourselves in his words about the necessity of completing in our own flesh the passion of Christ for the sake of his body, the church? Paul suffered every kind of trial and so leads us to ask, Do I follow Jesus in suffering, wherever he wants me to be, and where he goes before me and walks with me? Do I love him more than everything, as Paul did?

Aware of our own fragility, especially when measured against what the apostle Paul was in his mission as a preacher of the gospel, we pray in humble trust:

Lord Jesus Christ,
you are the Truth!
Enlighten us, we pray,
with the grace of your Spirit,
so that we may believe in the love
that appeared among us in you,
and so that we may wager our whole lives
on that love
like Paul,
the apostle of the gentiles.
You are the Way!
Guide us, we implore,
along the paths where
you, King-Servant out of love,

go before us and walk with us
in the grace of the Spirit
toward the Father's house,
as you guided the prisoner
of your love
to the supreme gift of his life.
You are the Life!
By your death
Death itself was vanquished,
by your resurrection
new life was born
for a world reconciled with God.
Let us live for you
and die for you,
so that, by the power of the holy Consoler,
we may one day glory
with Paul and all the saints
in your life without end.
Amen. Alleluia!

20

The Woman of the Apocalypse:
Lectio Divina on Revelation 12

The church will have fulfilled her mission when the Kingdom dawns in all its splendor over the horizon of history. Then the great battle joined in time will reach an end, and the victory of God, Lord of all things, will shine forth in the new heavens and new earth of the heavenly Jerusalem. This final battle and triumph of the Eternal One is the main focus of the author of the Book of Revelation; his purpose is to offer the fledgling Christian community — tested by the first signs of coming persecution and the growing controversy with the synagogue — an incontrovertible message of meaning and hope. Seen in this light, the Book of Revelation is really a kind of theology of hope under the guise of a theology of history; the drama of its words and visions in no way distracts from the message of faith in God's final victory that it wants to communicate or from the call to confidence that it extends to the disciples of the church of love in its own and every time.

In this context, particular importance is to be attributed to the Woman (12:1), the "great sign" who "appears" in the heavens (the form of the verb used here is *ōphthē*, characteristically employed for manifestations of the divine and for the appearances of the Risen Lord; cf. for example 1 Cor. 15:5-8). Counterposed to her is another figure, the Dragon (v. 3), no less fraught with symbolic significance, as is indicated by the use of the same verb *ōphthē*. This is "that ancient serpent, who is called the Devil and Satan, the deceiver of the whole world" (v. 9). The Woman flees to the desert, where God has prepared a refuge for her (v. 6), while the battle of

Michael and his angels against the Dragon continues (vv. 7-9); the Dragon is defeated and hurled to the earth, where he strikes out against the Woman and her descendants (vv. 13, 17). Mother and Son, however, will not succumb; they will instead be victorious (vv. 14, 16).

What does this epic, terrifying scenario signify? What is the meaning of the two opposing figures of the Woman and the Dragon? And what does their struggle mean, especially for the life and mission of the church in history? The Old Testament background of the passage helps us give an answer to these questions. First of all, there is the echo of Genesis 3:15, the text that proclaims the eternal enmity between the Woman and the serpent, between the serpent's seed and her seed, which will crush the head of the Beast. There are also reminiscences of the Exodus in the motif of the desert (v. 6) and of the eagles' wings given to the Woman so she could fly there (v. 14; cf. Exod. 19:4: "You have seen what I did to the Egyptians, and how I bore you on eagles' wings and brought you to myself"). The image of the dry earth that absorbs the waters of the river recalls the crossing of the Red Sea (vv. 15-16; cf. Exod. 14:22, 29). The image of the Woman in its turn evokes the New Jerusalem, mother of the messianic people (cf. Isa. 66:7) and mother of the chosen people, Israel (cf. Hos. 1–3; Isa. 26:17-18; Jer. 31:4, 15).

The Old Testament background thus clearly indicates that Revelation 12 should be read in terms of the coming of the Messiah in the last times, suggesting that we see in the Woman not only the expectant Israel of the Old Testament but also the Israel of the fulfillment, the new and definitive people of the covenant. This interpretation is confirmed by the way the Woman herself is presented: "clothed with the sun, with the moon under her feet, and on her head a crown of twelve stars" (v. 1). The sun is the source of light *par excellence*, an image of the sovereignty and transcendence of God, who is "wrapped in light as with a garment" (Ps. 104:2); the fact that she is clothed with the sun suggests that the Woman here stands for Zion, which will be clothed with "beautiful garments" (Isa. 52:1) and with "the garments of salvation" (Isa. 61:10) in the last days. Since the moon is the star on which the calendar is based (cf. Gen. 1:14-19), the fact that the Woman has the moon under her feet means that she is assured victory over the passage of the seasons; that is, she will not succumb to any earthly vicissitude. The crown of twelve stars, finally, recalls both the tribes of ancient Israel (cf. the dream of Joseph in Gen. 37:9) and "the twelve apostles of the Lamb" (Rev. 21:12, 14), the foundation of the new Jerusalem. This complex of symbols makes it even more appropriate to see in the Woman the image of the people of God of the two covenants.

The Woman gives birth to "a son, a male child, who is to rule all the nations with a rod of iron" (12:5). She is the Mother of the Messiah-King, who is generated in suffering — indicated by the fact that the Woman "was crying out in birth pangs, in the agony of giving birth" (v. 2) — and the object of the Dragon's ferocious opposition (v. 4b). Yet the Child is victorious, as shown by his being immediately "snatched away and taken to God and to his throne" (v. 5). What does this painful birth followed by immediate exaltation stand for? The connection among the birth pangs of the Woman, the opposition of the Beast, and the elevation of the Son evokes the paschal mystery; indeed, the fourth Gospel makes special use of the image of childbirth in speaking of how the disciples will pass from sadness to joy in their experience of the death and resurrection of the Lord (cf. John 16:21-23). In Revelation 12, the Woman who gives birth and her Son who is exalted are thus to be read as a symbol of the paschal victory over suffering and over the trials inflicted by the ancient Enemy.

So, bearing in mind this double symbolism of the Woman and of childbirth, the message of Revelation 12 may be formulated thus: in carrying out her mission in history, the church, the new Israel, experiences the pangs of giving birth and is the object of the Dragon's persecution; but, just as by his Passover the church's Lord has won victory over death and the Enemy, who is the Devil, so the Messiah's community will not succumb to these trials and will be saved by the power of him who already stands at the throne of God. The Easter triumph of the Son of the Woman is the anticipation and promise of the triumph of the church of the new covenant in the last days, even if at present she lives her mission out in the midst of the pangs of giving birth, crossing the "desert" in a time of testing and grace similar to Israel's exodus. The missionary activity of the people of God can thus be sustained by a hope stronger than any disappointment or defeat.

More specifically, however, the Woman who gives birth to the Messiah-King stands for Mary, the Mother of Jesus, called "woman" by John, both when he speaks of the Mother of Jesus standing at the foot of her Son's cross (John 19:25-27) and, earlier, when Jesus accomplishes the "first" of his signs at Cana, itself heavy with paschal significance (John 2:1-12). This reference to Mary confirms how the church — tested by the first signs of persecution — looked to the Mother of Jesus as a powerful image of the vocation and story of the whole of God's people, and thus found in her a source of comfort and hope in present suffering. In Mary, the church of the martyrs and pilgrims was able in substance to perceive her own destiny, entirely linked to Mary's Son, crucified and risen for humankind.

In the light of this understanding of the Woman of Revelation 12, of her Child, and of the Beast, we are also able to perceive the deep meaning of the place where all these things take place: the desert. Just as the echoes of Old Testament theology and spirituality are evident in this passage, so no less rich is the help they offer in interpreting those real-life situations in which the pilgrim church journeys toward the last things and is here and now engaged in the battle that will culminate in God's final victory. Bringing these Old Testament allusions together with the insights on Lady Church and Lady Mary in this passage, we can identify seven aspects of the symbol of the desert that speak to the life and mission of the community and of each disciple in the new and definitive covenant.

First of all, the desert is *the place for remembering love*. The Woman of the Apocalypse is called into the desert to be entirely enfolded there by the love of the Eternal One and so, in giving birth to the Son, to become the Mother of that love which receives and gives everything. This mystery of love, of which the desert speaks, has taken flesh in Mary, the Mother of the Messiah, who is at the same time the Woman of the battle of the last days; here the church learns to live out her mission in the desert of time by remaining ever mindful of the Trinity's initiative of love, letting herself be loved by God so as to become ever more capable of loving.

Second, for the Bible the desert is also *the place to listen to the Word* that saves. The rabbis liked to play on the similarity of sound between *dabar* and *midbar*, "word" and "desert," to express their conviction that only the Word can make the desert flower, and only in the desert can the Word sound out in all its creative power. The prophet Hosea echoes this tradition when he states, in his very beautiful song of the love between God and Israel: "Therefore, I will now allure her, and bring her into the wilderness, and speak tenderly to her" (2:14). At the heart of Jewish faith there is the call to listen — the *Shema* — and hence also that silence in which the Word comes, as in the desert, to call forth life. The desert stands for the silence where the Word dwells. Thus for the fathers Mary is the "desert in flower"; because she is the Virgin who listens, she is the silence in which the Word of God is spoken, the "desert" of human capabilities that lets itself be totally inhabited and molded by divine grace. From Mary — recognized in the Woman of the Apocalypse, led into the desert — the church learns how an attitude of attentive and fruitful listening has to be at the foundation of mission, in that contemplative condition that alone creates preparedness for the eschatological battle and leads to a sharing in the victory of God.

Third, the desert is further understood in the Bible as *the place of testing*. In Deuteronomy it is written: "Do not exalt yourself, forgetting the Lord your God, who brought you out of the land of Egypt, out of the house of slavery, who led you through the great and terrible wilderness. . . . He made water flow for you from the flint rock; and fed you in the wilderness with manna that your ancestors did not know, to humble you and to test you, and in the end to do you good" (8:14-16). These words recall the trials experienced by Israel in her Exodus journey, but they can also be applied to the terrible trials involved in the attack that, according to Revelation, the Beast will let loose on the Woman in the desert: in both cases, the waters stand both for danger and — when they withdraw — for the way to salvation. In her turn, Mary experienced the testing of faith (cf. the sword of which Luke 2:35 speaks) right up to the foot of the cross (John 19:25-27). From her we learn to bear trials, trusting in God and his fidelity, crossing the desert in all its ambiguity as the place both of refuge and of struggle, where we experience both the protection of the Most High and the ferocity of the voracious Dragon.

Fourth, biblical tradition also presents the desert as *the place of God's fidelity*. Once again, the Book of Deuteronomy assures us that it is in the desert that Israel experiences the faithfulness of the Most High:

> He sustained him in a desert land,
> in a howling wilderness waste;
> he shielded him, cared for him,

> guarded him as the apple of his eye.
> As an eagle stirs up its nest,
>> and hovers over its young;
> as it spreads its wings, takes them up,
>> and bears them aloft on its pinions,
> the Lord alone guided him;
>> no foreign god was with him.   (32:10-12)

Like Israel, the Woman of the Apocalypse experiences God's tender protection, the Eternal One's faithfulness to the covenant, in the desert. In her turn, Mary, Mother of the Messiah, celebrates the wonders accomplished by this faithful God: her *Magnificat* teaches us to believe in the impossible possibilities created by God in every situation. These insights help the church grow in the certainty of never being left to herself in the trials she experiences as she lives out her mission. Her Lord takes care of her; right there, in the midst of the challenges of mission, he manifests the inexhaustible reserves of his faithfulness to his people.

Fifth, the tradition of the faith also perceives the desert as *the place not so much of human absence as of divine presence.* The whole story of the Exodus shows how it was in the desert that Israel learned to walk together as a people guided by her God. Acts also presents the community journeying in the desert as an image of the church of the pilgrims of God (cf. Acts 7:30, 36, 38). The Woman of the Apocalypse, led into the desert, is in her turn an image of Israel and of the church; as such, she speaks of the impossibility of any separation between the desert and the people of the covenant. Mary, image of the church that is Virgin and Mother, teaches us how to be the church of love, experiencing the desert not as human absence but as the living presence of our God.

Sixth, the desert is no less *the place to experience our yearning for the face of God.* As the psalmist in Psalm 63 prays:

> O God, you are my God, I seek you,
>> my soul thirsts for you;
> my flesh faints for you,
>> as in a dry and weary land where there is no water.   (vv. 1-2)

In Psalm 143 the thirsty aridity of the desert itself is the symbol of the longing for God:

> I stretch out my hands to you;
>> my soul thirsts for you like a parched land.   (v. 6)

The Woman of the Apocalypse is led into the desert to be nourished there by the Eternal One, signifying the hunger and thirst that only he can satisfy. Mary, the Mother of Jesus, is in her turn the woman of faith, the believer who walks toward the hidden Face and teaches us always to yearn for the vision of that divine Countenance in humble and trusting faith in the Most High. Drawing on this wealth of symbolism, the church learns to live out her own mission while thirsting for God, crossing the deserts of time in search of his Face that alone can satisfy our longings.

Finally, the desert is *the place where the eighth day is prepared.* The fact that Revelation situates the final battle in this desert landscape underlines the relationship between the desert and the fulfillment of history in God. St. Jerome celebrates this: "O desert full of the flowers of Christ! O solitude generating the stones meant for the building of the great King's city as foreseen in the vision of the Apocalypse! O hermitage where we can enjoy intimacy with God."[6] With the Woman of the final battle we discover the desert as the place to remember the end, to look forward to the last times. With Mary, Mother of the new and last Adam, we learn to live out our struggle against the Enemy, and to draw into the human present the future of God's promise.

The wealth of symbolism condensed in the image of the Woman of the Apocalypse and of the battle engaged by her and her Son against the Beast thus helps us recognize our pilgrim vocation of God's people as we journey homeward. And so we ask: How do we live in our own desert? Is it for us the place to remember the love of the living God? Is it a place to listen, where the Word makes the parched earth flower into God's marvelous garden, growing in every human heart and in the heart of history? Is it a place of testing, discovered in our daily struggle for fidelity? Is it the

---

6. St. Jerome, *Epistula 14.*

178

place where we experience the faithful God, who never abandons his people as they do battle with the Enemy? Is our desert not so much a matter of human absence as of divine presence, and so the place of a charity that is ever new and faithful? Is it the school where we learn to thirst for the hidden Countenance, where our longing for the Most High is nourished and shared? Is it the place where we experience in advance the eighth day, that radiant, splendid day when the desert will flower forever, and victory in the last battle will be assured to the living God, all in all, God of our hope that is stronger than suffering and death?

Turning to Mary, Mother of the Lord, Woman of the eighth day, trusting in the help of her maternal intercession, we ask the grace to live out our mission both as individuals and as church in this exodus of time, pilgrims of hope and credible witnesses of charity and faith. And we do this in the words of a woman, Vittoria Colonna (1490-1547), who invoked Mary thus, as star of the sea of life and of history:

> Bright star mirrored in our sea, you who are
> so secure, the true sun whose flesh you made
> makes you beautiful — your virginity
> augured, gave such sweet shades, to His Light as
>
> it appeared on earth, to His innocence.
> Those who gaze on you, on your wonder, care
> nothing for this venal world, feel nothing
> but contempt for the vain godless quarrels
>
> of old enemies; your victory arms
> us with goodness and strength. Here God's son at
> a virgin mother's breast, there together
>
> magnificently clothed in Paradise.
> Stirred by boundless serenity, my wish,
> eager need's content: I serve faithfully.[7]

7. Vittoria Colonna, "Stella del nostro mar chiara e secura" (trans. Ellen Moody).

Sixth Day

CONCLUSION

21

John, Contemplating Love

As our traveling companion for this last stretch of our exercises we choose John the apostle, the "contemplative of love." Precisely because of the central place occupied in his teaching by the experience and proclamation of God's love, he can help us move from this time of special grace to the "daily" grace of time, in which we are called to live as disciples of love in the church of the Trinity at the service of the women and men of today.

The full identity of the author of the fourth Gospel is shrouded in a considerable degree of discretion: the final verses of chapter 21 (vv. 20-24) identify him as the "disciple whom Jesus loved . . . the one who had reclined next to Jesus at the supper and had said, 'Lord, who is it that is going to betray you?'" (v. 20). Of him, Peter asks Jesus: "Lord, what about him?" And Jesus replies: "If it is my will that he remain until I come, what is that to you?" (vv. 21, 22). Jesus here does not mean that this disciple will not die (v. 23), but that he is *par excellence* the disciple who knows what it is to yearn to meet his Beloved Master, who has gone to prepare a place for us in the Father's heart.

He is clearly one of the three disciples closest to the Lord — Peter, James, and John. He is not Peter, in that he is mentioned as being in the latter's company (as in the visit to the tomb on the morning of the day after the Sabbath; John 20:2-10); and he is not James, who died very soon after Jesus' death and resurrection, in about AD 44, executed by the sword at Herod's behest, as Acts 12:2 tells us. Consequently he must be John. The very fact that he is thus shrouded in discretion and silence already gives us some idea of the kind of person he was: the contemplative of love, traditionally identified as the youngest of the disciples, in part because he has all those characteristics of audacity and tenderness which the young especially tend to possess. It is also significant that he is the only one of the disciples who remains at the foot of the cross with the Mother of Jesus; thus, too, he shows himself to be the disciple of love, the beloved.

John is the son of Zebedee and brother of James, and he comes from Galilee, where the two brothers were partners in a small fishing business with two other brothers, Simon and Andrew. John had probably first been a disciple of the Baptist, and he might have been one of the two disciples who were with the Baptist when the latter pointed out Jesus, who was walking by, as the Lamb of God (John 1:35-36). The two then followed Jesus, after having asked him, "Rabbi, where are you staying?" and having been invited by the Lord to follow him even before they had seen: "Come and see" (John 1:38-39). Of the two, he would obviously have to be the one whose name is not mentioned, since the other is certainly Andrew, who immediately afterward went to call his brother Simon. Even though John is so reserved in the way he writes about himself, we are still able to identify his main characteristics and the most significant moments in the story of his faith in, and love for, the Christ: his call, his intimacy with the Master, his being the one to receive the Lord's last will and testament, the witness he bears to the resurrection, the fact that he was in a special way the disciple who experienced a longing for Jesus' return, and his particularly intense contemplation of God's love.

First, his *call*, described against the backdrop of the opening week of the fourth Gospel, evidently modeled on the week of creation in Genesis 1:

> The next day John again was standing with two of his disciples, and as he watched Jesus walk by, he exclaimed, "Look, here is the Lamb of God!" The two disciples heard him say this, and they followed Jesus. When Jesus turned and saw them following, he said to them, "What are you looking for?" They said to him, "Rabbi" (which translated means Teacher), "where are you staying?" He said to them, "Come and see." They came and saw where he was staying, and they remained with him

that day. It was about four o'clock in the afternoon [literally: "the tenth hour"]. (John 1:35-39)

John is introduced here as a person in search of God: he had gone to the Baptist, evidently moved by his thirst for the Eternal One, and, when the Baptist pointed to Jesus as the Lamb of God, he had no hesitation in leaving his master and following the Nazarene. The question, "Master, where are you staying?" speaks of his longing to stay with Jesus. John had understood that to follow Jesus was to find the true home of his life. The Master responds by inviting him to have confidence, to believe without seeing: "Come and see." In matters of faith, when we contemplate the mystery, seeing comes after we have abandoned ourselves entirely: first one comes, and then one sees! This is what the two disciples in fact do; and such is the impression left on them by meeting Jesus, a meeting that will mark their lives forever, that John remembers the exact time it took place with the chronological exactitude so typical of the memory we have of the times of a great love: "It was about four o'clock in the afternoon" (v. 39). To be called is to meet Someone, not something, and it is the desire to follow the One who changes your life, so that you can stay with him and live in him.

At the dramatic moment when Judas is about to betray Jesus, John's second characteristic, *his intimacy with Jesus,* becomes especially evident. This is the hour of supreme love ("he loved them to the end") and of the bitterest sorrow ("his hour had come"; John 13:1). John is the one who stays closer to Jesus than any of the others, and so his life demonstrates how faith and love are inseparable, as are love and suffering, closeness to the Beloved and sharing in his suffering. The evidence of his love is there for all to see: he is the beloved disciple, the image of every disciple who loves, who reclines against Jesus' bosom (v. 23: *en tō kolpō*), just as the Son always lives and moves in the Father's embrace (cf. John 1:18: *eis ton kolpon*). It is in reply to a question from John that Jesus reveals the identity of the one who is to betray him, but who continues to be loved by Jesus, as indicated by the fact that the Master gives Judas the piece of bread (v. 26: a gesture indicative of special love), the bread that will accompany Judas even into the night, and will not leave him (v. 30: Judas takes the piece of bread with him). Love never abandons the beloved, even when the beloved is unfaithful; even the one who flees from love bears love's pledge with him, thus rendering evident the paradox of a love that is stronger than betrayal and death. Against this backdrop of Jesus' love, which is stronger than any other thing, John's trust in, and intimacy with, the Master are especially clear: faith is being so much in love with God as to enter into an ever deeper relationship with him, a relationship of complete honesty, in the unblemished transparency of suffering and love.

In the intensely moving scene of the exchange between John and Jesus while the beloved disciple stands next to Jesus' Mother at the foot of the cross (John 19:26-27), we see John's third main characteristic: John is portrayed as the *one who receives the Lord's last will and testament*. This is when everything comes to fulfillment. In this highest and most final of hours, John alone among the disciples stayed with Mary by the cross. The words Jesus says are like the last will of the abandoned Prophet, who turns to the "woman," his Mother, the image here of Israel and the church, and to the disciple of love, the image of every disciple, and establishes between them a relationship of such depth that the disciple takes the woman into his heart of hearts. In his last will, Jesus leaves the beloved disciple three treasures: Israel, the church, and his Mother. The disciple of love will love Israel, the "holy root," as Jesus has loved her; he will love the church as the fruit borne by Jesus' passion; he will love Jesus' Mother as his own. The crucified Lord thus places his disciple within a network of loving relationships, which at the same time he entrusts to his care. To have faith, to believe, is to have a heart ready to welcome covenants of peace and bonds of unity and to live these out in daily faithfulness and in obedience to the crucified Lord. "When Jesus saw his mother and the disciple whom he loved standing beside her, he said to his mother, 'Woman, here is your son.' Then he said to the disciple, 'Here is your mother.' And from that hour the disciple took her into his own home" (19:26-27).

The beloved disciple is, fourthly, also a *special witness of the resurrection*, as is demonstrated by the episode of the visit paid by him to the tomb, in the company of Peter, on Easter morning (John 20:1-8). John runs to see Jesus: he is moved by a yearning born of love, which is longing, desire, hope against all hope, even against the brutal evidence of death's final silence. He gets to the tomb first, but he waits: he knows the respect that love creates and that is able to stand aside to make room for the other person, in this case for the disciple to whom Jesus has especially entrusted his church. John sees the tomb empty and believes: his faith is able to grasp what his eyes do not see; his faith is able to read the absence of the Beloved's body as a word more eloquent than any presence. It is precisely thus that the beloved disciple becomes the eyewitness, the one who has seen and can thus pass on to others the love that opens the eyes of faith and allows them to perceive the Lord's presence: this is what he movingly declares at the beginning of the first letter that bears his name, the "letter of love" (cf. 1 John 1:1-4). Those who have experienced and seen and touched the Beloved cannot keep him for themselves; they become his witnesses, in love with him and radiating their love of him to others. Faith comes to life in a love that shares.

And yet this disciple who witnesses to the presence of the Risen Lord here and now continues to be the *disciple full of longing,* his fifth characteristic. We are helped to understand how this can be so by the mysterious exchange between Jesus and Peter concerning John, in the concluding, additional chapter of the fourth Gospel:

> Peter turned and saw the disciple whom Jesus loved following them; he was the one who had reclined next to Jesus at the supper and had said, "Lord, who is it that is going to betray you?" When Peter saw him, he said to Jesus, "Lord, what about him?" Jesus said, "If it is my will that he remain until I come, what is that to you? Follow me!" So the rumor spread in the community that this disciple would not die. Yet Jesus did not say to him that he would not die, but "If it is my will that he remain until I come, what is that to you?" This is the disciple who is testifying to these things and has written them, and we know that his testimony is true. (John 21:20-24)

From this exchange emerges a special characteristic of the beloved disciple: John is the one who awaits the return of Jesus. The disciple of love leans forward in hope toward the joy of the face-to-face meeting. In him, the memory of the Beloved is not nostalgia or regret, but tenderness, hope, vigilance, and expectation. Love does not live in the past but opens out toward the future and draws that future into the present by its own very ardor. Faith is neither grasping nor possession, but continual desire, incessant thirst, unremitting search for the hidden Countenance. Whoever believes needs a continual encounter with the Beloved, continual prayer, and so faith is a journey in the night guided by the Star of redemption toward the dawn, glimpsed but not yet fully seen in the bright day of God.

Taking these different traits together, John truly emerges as the *contemplative of love,* his final characteristic. The book of Revelation explicitly confirms this, in presenting the visions and words of hope of the infant church as the direct testimony of the beloved disciple (cf. Rev. 1:9-19). John is old by now, and he lives deep in God. He writes of himself as a brother and companion to all who bear tribulation out of their faithful love for Jesus. He lives in the joy of liturgical encounter: it is the Lord's Day, and he is taken up in ecstasy in the Spirit. He *sees* the voice: as only the contemplative can, he sees by listening; the words of revelation become something he sees; he understands through symbols and savors the things of God.

And the revelation he sees is a mighty message of conversion, consolation, and hope for the "seven churches," which stand for the whole church in every time and place (the number seven indicates perfection and fullness), and which are tested by outward persecution (by the Romans, but also by the synagogue) and by the inner trial of faith, in what many consider an intolerable delay in the Lord's coming. The disciple of love, rich in years and the experience of faith, knows how to direct his own and others' eyes to the Lamb who stands sacrificed, to Christ died and risen from the dead; he teaches how present trials are nothing other than the way to wash one's garments in the blood of the Lamb and so enter with him into glory. The faith of the disciple of love leads into the hope of victorious love and of the joy that never sets in the heavenly Jerusalem: "The one who testifies to these things says, 'Surely I am coming soon.' Amen. Come, Lord Jesus" (Rev. 22:20).

So John, this contemplative of love, challenges all of us who are called to be disciples and, like him, contemplatives of love and witnesses of yearning, industrious in charity and ardent in faith; and he poses questions that engage us in an evaluation of how we follow the Master: Am I ready to respond to Jesus' call to "come and see," or do I insist on seeing before abandoning myself to him? Do I love the Lord? Do I let him love me? Do I live out my love for Christ in my love for others and for the church? Do I bear witness to my Beloved? Is the yearning for God and for his countenance alive in me? Do I have the hope that comes from a love that is able to wait and pray? Do I share hope with others even in the darkest hours of life and history? Do I nourish myself with God, his Word, his silence, the grace of his sacraments, and the strength of his love received and given, at every moment of my life, no matter the ups and downs of seasons and times? Am I faithful in consolation, as well as in the unavoidable times of desolation?

A great contemplative of love, St. John of the Cross, who knew well the divine light but also the night of the soul, helps us to respond to these questions, entering into the attitude of contemplation, which, even though it is nighttime, does not let go of the source of light, but recognizes its rays and lets itself be filled with them ever more:

How well I know that fountain's rushing flow
Although by night

Its deathless spring is hidden. Even so
Full well I guess from whence its source flow
Though it be night.

Its origin (since it has none) none knows:
But that all origin from it arose
Although by night.

I know there is no other thing so fair
And earth and heaven drink refreshment there
Although by night.

Full well I know the depth no man can sound
And that no ford to cross it can be found
Though it be night

Its clarity unclouded still shall be:
Out of it comes the light by which we see
Though it be night.

Flush with its banks the stream so proudly swells;
I know it waters nations, heavens, and hells
Though it be night.

The current that is nourished by this source
I know to be omnipotent in force
Although by night.[1]

---

1. St. John of the Cross, "Que bien sé yo la fonte" (trans. Roy Campbell).